Tied in Knots

3 Steps to Releasing Stress

Mary Jane Cronin

Published by WiggleBug Publishing

Edited by Robin Powell and Margaret McMullen

Cover Art by Scott Howard @MyScottArt

Library of Congress Number Pending

Dedication

This book is dedicated to all those who, like me, have experienced stress in their lives. Those who unselfishly gave to others without resting or recharging themselves. It is my wish that with this book, you will continue to help others in a healthier way. Thank you!

To my sons, Jaime, Jesse, and Johnathan who may have caused me stress while growing up, but who also helped me de-stress when I needed it. Thank you!

To my guardian angel, my son, Jeremy who sends me signs and messages from heaven that calm me, inspire me to continue to help others and to make me smile. Thank you!

Acknowledgments

There is a saying that we learn from our mistakes and difficult times. I believe this to be true. Situations, events, and people in my life have resulted in my learning ways to release my stress and to now share them with you.

The list of people who offered to generously share their stories of how they released stress is amazing, I wish to acknowledge and thank them. Ashley Kraus, Baran Ayoub, Brandt DeForest, Heather Sullivan, Jennifer Zibell, Kerry Brown, Linda Burhans, Renee Mendoza, Robin Riddell, Ron Regen, and Stephannie Maki. Thank you.

Contents

Introduction

People experience and respond to stress in different ways. One reason for this is due to a person's personality. What's stressful to one person may be all in a day's work for another. People with "Type A" personalities, and "Type B" personalities handle stress differently.

One's goals and the importance placed on them can also affect reactions to stress. Many people live their lives filled with obligations and demands from others. Work demands and home-life demands are frequently in conflict resulting in stress.

Having coping skills before a potential stressful situation arises, works to reduce or prevent the stress.

In writing this book, I hope to help you find the answers to the questions of what is needed to cope with a situation, and do you have the resources needed to cope.

ARE YOU STRESSED?

How many of you get stressed? Me too. In fact, stress has become a worldwide epidemic with no sign of slowing down. Resulting from family, home, environmental, or one's job, it is a part of most peoples' lives. Stress can have a positive affect when it creates an adrenaline rush or sense of accomplishment.

Negative stress, however causes physical, emotional and mental disruptions. This negative stress, that many people experience on the job is the reason for my writing this book.

Everyone who has ever held a job has, at some point, felt the pressure of work-related stress. Suzie, an employee at a large non-profit agency worked with several nurses who shared that they were under enormous pressures.

She knew that health care professionals, employees, and family caregiver's all work in potentially draining environments. These workers may be prone to work-related stress, burnout, and decline in job performance.

What was a surprising realization was that while some employees did suffer while performing their duties, others flourished under that same pressure. Suzie began to see that stress is a highly personalized phenomenon, and can vary widely, even in identical situations for different reasons.

Coping skills such as positive thinking and learning cognitive behaviors can result in an increased sense of well-being, better physical health, job longevity and decrease in stress.

Make no mistake, any job can have stressful elements, even if you love what you do. In the short-term, you may experience pressure to meet a deadline or to fulfill a difficult obligation. However, when work stress becomes chronic, it can be overwhelming — and harmful to both physical and emotional health.

The American Psychological Association's annual Stress in America survey has consistently found that work is listed as a significant source of stress by the majority of Americans.

Work-related stress doesn't just disappear when you head home for the day. When stress persists, it can take a toll on your home life, relationships, your health and well-being.

After talking with her friends, Suzie began doing some research to evaluate her own life and what part stress played in her job performance and well-being.

While at work the following day, Suzie found herself nervously tapping her fingers on the table. This was always a warning sign that she was beginning to feel stressed. Through the years, she had come to recognize her symptoms, but not the triggers that caused her to feel stressed. When stressed, her brain found it hard to concentrate, she became irritable, and just like today, the finger tapping would start.

How many times had she said to herself, "I'm feeling so stressed today"? Too many to count for sure, but today, she decided to do something about it.

Suzie told a co-worker, Alex that she felt like she was the only person on the planet who got stressed out. Listening empathetically, he asked what is stress? She was surprised at the question, but explained,

"Stress is the body's emotional or physical reaction to harmful situations. Situations, whether they're real or perceived, or some spontaneous changes in our lives".

When you feel threatened, a chemical reaction occurs in your body that allows you to act in a certain way to prevent injury.

Alex then asked her when she felt stressed the most. Susie replied, "I get stressed whenever I get scared, overwhelmed, or if something changes in my day without me having time to prepare for it". Looking around at others in the office that day, she knew deep down inside that it wasn't true. Other people got stressed too.

She wanted to find out what stressed others out and most importantly, what they did to stop those feelings. That day, Suzie decided to begin her quest to learn more about stress.

First stop was the Google site on the internet. Typing in the word "stress" produced over 35 million results. Such a large number confirmed that she indeed, was not the only stressed person.

She read that stress can come from something that frightens, confuses, irritates, or even excite us. Reading some statistics, she discovered eighty percent of all people said they were stressed at some time in their lives. The majority of them said work or home life stressed them out the most.

In 2013 a survey was completed by more than 1,200 adult Americans, and the findings were...stressful. The average person reported over 2,000 hours of feeling stressed every year. If laid out in a row, they would average out to each person feeling stressed for eighty-three non-stop days.

Suzie could relate to those statistics. Being a mom, an employee, and someone caring for her elderly mother, there was little time spent relaxing or unwinding.

From her research, Suzie found that when asked, most Americans said they spent at least half of their day-to-day life stressed out. Only nine percent reported feeling happy during their average workday.

Turning off the computer and equipped with these statistics, Suzie began reflecting on her own work life. She made a list of the things she liked about her job and the things that frustrated her and made her feel stressed.

Suzie admitted she liked the money that she made. Having been employed with the same company for a while now had some special perks. The raises she received over the years had not only helped her pay her bills, but it enabled her to buy a newer car. Not having the stress of worrying if her car would start each morning was a blessing. She liked the place she worked and got along with most of her co-workers but there were some negatives as well.

Some days when she went to work the air conditioning was so cold that she had to wear a coat. Although she did get along with most of her co-workers, there was that one person who talked loudly and laughed at his own jokes. Both of these occurrences resulted in a lack of concentration for her.

This current stress, unhappiness and over all thought of "I can't wait for this workday to be over" attitude was felt by seventy-three percent of those questioned.

The location of where you live and work can also play a role in your productiveness and happiness at work. People who lived in California stated they felt less stressed and experienced little anxiety compared to the group from New York City. Having said that, some people do indeed like the hustle and bustle of a more intense work place and would be bored with a calmer environment. The goal is to find a job and location where you feel comfortable and are challenged.

Suzie started thinking back to a commercial she saw when she was a teenager. In the commercial a woman sitting in a bathtub said "Calgon, take me away." The commercial gave the impression that a soak in the tub would give you quiet time and reduce stress. The commercial was partly true. She agreed with that idea.

The majority of women surveyed said what they needed most was a good, old-fashion "take me away" vacation. If a vacation wasn't possible, at least more personal time to themselves.

Stressful situations can be real or perceived because the mind doesn't know the difference. This is why you may feel stressed following a car accident you were involved in, and also when you're re-telling the story of that accident.

When talking about your experience, the mind doesn't know if it's real or not. The mind just knows how thinking about it makes you feel. Whenever you feel threatened, scared or uncomfortable, a chemical reaction occurs in your body that conditions you to react in a certain way to prevent potential injury.

This reaction is known as the Fight or Flight response.

As stated, most people feel stressed from time to time, but some people cope more effectively or recover from these stressful events quicker than others. The challenge is to learn their secrets of how to reduce our stress.

"We can easily manage if we will only take, each day, the burden appointed to it. But the load will be too heavy for us if we carry yesterday's burden over again today, and then add the burden of tomorrow before we are required to bear it."   John Newton

Something that causes us stress can be a one-time event, a short-term occurrence, or an incident that continues to happen over a long period of time.

Our bodies are designed and conditioned to handle small doses of stress. They are however, not equipped to handle long-term, repeated chronic stress without having negative consequences.

Suzie checked out a book from the library about the different type of stress people experience. She learned there are four types of stress. The most common form of stress is called acute stress. This type of stress can be exciting in small doses, but too much of it can become exhausting.

Thinking back to a vacation she took where she went skiing, she understood acute stress. The first few times she took a fast run down a challenging slope were exhilarating. The feel of the wind hitting her face and the uncertainty and excitement of completing it without falling was her goal. Although the challenge to complete the run remained the same, later in the day, the run became draining and no longer anticipated.

Acute stress can also be produced by negative events. It's the flat tire on your way to work, the loss of an important contract, a deadline you are rushing to meet, or even your child's occasional problems at school.

Fortunately, because it is short term, acute stress doesn't have enough time to do the extensive damage associated with long-term stress. This fight-or-flight response, may actually be helpful in a life-threatening situation, or, in an exhilarating situation such as bungee jumping or sky diving.

Chronic stress however, is the type of stress many are warned to reduce in their lives. It results from internal or external pressures suffered for a prolonged period of time. In these situations, an individual perceives that they have little or no control. Chronic stress often occurs from everyday stressors that are ignored for too long or are poorly managed.

The consequences of chronic stress are serious, particularly because it contributes to anxiety and depression. People who suffer from depression and anxiety, are at two times the risk for heart disease than people without these conditions.

Environmental conditions such as lighting, smells, or the coldness of Suzie's working environment may be simply annoying at first. When they happen time and time again, they may soon result in health issues such as more frequent colds and lack of productivity due to reduced concentration.

Emotional stress can be particularly painful and challenging to deal with as well. This type of stress involves both the mind and heart. Relationship stress carries a heavy toll on our emotional lives and creates strong responses.

Our relationships with family, friends or even co-workers can greatly impact our lives, both for the better or for worse.

Conflicted relationships and 'frenemies' (friends we have a positive and negative relationship with) can make us feel worse off emotionally and take a toll on us physically and mentally.

One of the significant reasons we experience emotional stress is our human need to feel "part of" something other than ourselves. This need may or may not be fulfilled, or when younger, may have been removed from our lives.

Suzie realized she had a lack of self confidence in herself since childhood. She was always chubby and was often picked last for outdoor games during recess. Told by teachers of the team "lucky" enough to get her.

The lack of self-confidence and insecurity she felt as a child, followed her through adulthood and caused her to become isolated at work and in her personal life. Isolation can be caused by friends, acquaintances, co-workers, family or even strangers. No matter the source, being excluded or ignored affects us and still can hurt us emotionally.

Burnout, the final stage of stress is defined by Merriam Webster dictionary as "exhaustion of physical or emotional strength or motivation, usually as a result of prolonged stress or frustration." This often happens when continued chronic stress continues and shows no sign of being resolved. Burnout often develops in situations that leave people feeling they have a lack of control in their lives to change things.

High levels of demands from others, or unclear expectations, lack of recognition for achievements, or an increased level of risk or negative consequences when mistakes are made, can all contribute to burnout.

Was Suzie at risk for burnout at work from stress?

She began evaluating her reactions to the stress in her she was just imagining this happening didn't help. Even now, she could still close her eyes and remember the looks of displeasure on the member's faces life. She discovered she called in sick to work more often lately than she had in the past. Finding when she woke with headaches, or had trouble sleeping, she convinced herself sliding back under the covers was a better solution. She was once a top employee, but admitted her heart was no longer in it.

Looking back, things began to change when she had been reprimanded in front of her co-workers for getting a report turned in late. Being scolded in front of others made her feel embarrassed and afraid to face her fellow employees.

While at the library doing her research, Suzie came across a small book called Zugg's Stress Experiences. Zugg was an advanced caveman who had learned to survive by hunting, using tools and building shelters for others in his village. One day while in the woods, Zugg heard a twig snap.

The last time he heard a twig snap sound like that, it was from a wild animal who came out of the underbrush and ate his sister Zuggina.

Since that terrible day, whenever he heard a twig snapping, his mind raced back to that day with his sister, and he associated the sound with wild animals and without hesitation or thinking...he prepared for battle. Focusing his mind to the area of the snapping sound, he was filled with fear and anger. He wondered if he would have to fight this unseen wild animal today or if he had time to escape.

With his heart racing, adrenaline and sugar entered his body as it prepared for battle. When preparing for this battle, blood was taken from unimportant areas such as digestion, healing infections and body wounds, and now went to muscles of the arms and legs and his trunk area for strength. His eyes narrowed and his muscles tensed...he was ready to battle the beast or use those muscles to get to a safe place.

As Suzie reached the last page of the book, she began to think about the four types of stress and how they had affected Zugg.

Zugg experienced acute stress when he heard a twig snap while hunting. Following that one day's events, every time he heard a twig snap, his mind went back to that horrible day.

As a result of doing this, he developed chronic stress that over time reduced his abilities. Every time he went hunting or was in that underbrush, he thought of his sister. Zugg's emotional stress arose whenever he thought of his sister's death. He then became tearful and the fear of his own life possibly ending the same way returned.

Zugg soon became the victim of his burnout. Burnout resulted in his not wanting to leave his home. He didn't want to experience those same feeling of sadness, the fear, and the stress of hunting anymore.

But we are not Zugg. He was able to hunt and build houses to work off his stress, or distract his stress by looking for food. When we get stressed, our stress often has nowhere to go and continues to build up inside us.

This can become a problem

You see, we are really no different from Zugg. We all have responsibilities and obligations to meet. One of Zugg's responsibilities, like most of us, was to provide for his family. He was doing this through hunting and gathering and building villager's homes. Just like us, when he was experiencing those unforeseen events, he felt stressed.

Maybe in looking at Zugg and Suzie's stress situations, we can find solutions and coping skills to reduce the effect of stress in our own lives.

Which of these situations are stressful to you?

- You receive a promotion at work.

- Your car has a flat tire.

- You go to a party that ends at 2: a.m.

- Your dog gets sick.

For some people going to a party until 2am sounds exciting and fun. For others, the thought of loud noise and being around many people can stress them out. As you can see, stress affects different people differently.

If you asked most people what emotion they would like to do without, most likely they would say stress as their least favorite. That may be because they are not thinking of good stress.

Positive stress can also help our brain to focus.

Positive, or good stress might actually improve some facets of our brains. In some instances, stress is actually a reasoning enhancer which can help us in professional capacities.

Stress is created to help us react to potentially dangerous situations in the wild. For instance, when trying to escape from a potential burglar, it would not be advantageous to be thinking about stopping at the store after work to buy food for dinner that night. We need to focus on what is important at the time.

Stress helps you narrow your attention and to focus on the task at hand. Stress has also been shown in some studies to help increase memory and recall in our brain when we are experiencing stress.

This is due to a slightly higher levels of cortisol, a steroid hormone that is released by the adrenal gland in response to stress. Not only does stress release higher levels of cortisol, it also releases higher levels of adrenaline which speeds up your heart rate and your metabolism.

When we think of stressful events, we tend to think of examples such as college exams, going to an interview or giving a speech. This is partly why we think of stress as entirely a bad thing. Negative stress such as working too many hours or having a leaky roof can be detrimental to your health. Situations that produce bad stress are generally considered unpleasant.

Stress however, in the right circumstances can be a good thing and create challenges, suspense and excitement. Good stress is stress that accompanies a situation that is positive, motivates us or has positive benefits.

> The irony is this: Our bodies react to stress in exactly the same way whether or not we have a good reason for being stressed. The body doesn't care if we're right or wrong. Even in those times when we feel perfectly justified in getting angry - when we tell ourselves it's the healthy response - we pay for it just the same.
> Doc Childre and Howard Martin

Suzie thought back to her most productive days at work. She realized the excitement and anticipation of being employee of the month had increased her performance and endurance. The dose of good stress helped fight her tiredness and fatigue.

Thinking of the most important and happiest moments of her life, Suzie saw they were also very stressful. The first day on her new job, her wedding, marriage, and her first child were all surrounded with good stress.

Suzie's realized that although these situations were probably all highly stressful, instead of being negative changes, they represented exciting positive life changes in her life. So, you see, not all stress is bad.

What are some of your positive stressors?

←————————————————————————→

What are some of your negative stressors?

Stressors can be both good and bad. Children can be a positive or a negative stressor in your life. When they achieve an award and make you proud, that is a positive stress. However, when they miss curfew and you're wondering where they are, fear and anger take over and you experience negative stress.

Work is one of the environments that can be a good and bad stressor. Working towards an upcoming deadline can cause some people to develop an adrenaline rush and work harder. For others, that upcoming deadline caused them negative stress and may result in mistakes and worry about finishing in time.

Now that Suzie understood what stress was, and that there was good and bad stress, she wondered what it was doing to her mind, body and spirit to remain stressed.

WHAT'S WRONG WITH A LITTLE STRESS?

Today we don't have to worry about wild animals like Zugg did, but we do face deadlines, emotional conflicts and financial pressures. Our bodies are conditioned to react to the stress of today the same way as our caveman ancestor.

When we get prepared for battle and do not fight, we are left with a fully-charged body that does not relax. Although we do have wild animal instincts, the need for daily battle is gone and we often remain stressed.

This instinct has been instilled in mankind from the years of Zugg.

Someone cuts you off in traffic, you lose a file in your computer, or your roof begins to leak and your reflexes kick in, and you are ready to battle. This causes us to walk around fully charged and often walk around filled with bottled up energy which is unhealthy.

When experiencing stress our minds and emotions may become distorted. Not everyone experiences stress symptoms, but for those do, developing tools to manage that stress can reduce or eliminate them.

Do you have any Emotional and Cognitive Symptoms?

Feeling irritable at little things	Having memory problems	Finding it hard to make decisions
Feeling restless	Not having enough energy	Having emotional outbursts
Feeling frustrated at having to wait	Thinking about negative things	Negative self-talk

Suzie now knew a little more about stress and she wondered to herself, "What symptoms could she have been experiencing, that without knowing it, could be due to stress"?

Stress at home or at work can produce emotional or cognitive symptoms.

Suzie realized her lack of energy and negative thoughts or self-talk could be from workplace stress.

No longer laughing at jokes shared by others and feeling frustrated at having to wait for other employees to complete their part of a joint task were possibly an outcome of chronic work conditions. Suzie was often unable to concentrate on her job requirements and forgot important deadlines.

Stress did not just surface at work for Suzie, there were signs at home as well. Feeling irritable and restless after work may have been from not decompressing after a stressful day at work.

In the evenings she would often eat too much and have mood swings that produced emotional outburst while watching Hallmark movies. The lives of the people in the movie seemed so calm. They all appeared so happy and every problem was rectified within the ninety minutes.

Do you have any Physical Symptoms?

Muscle tension	Stomach/abdominal pain	Shortness of breath
Low back pain	Muscle spasms or nervous tics	Too little or too much sleep
Pains in chest	Sweating when not physically active	Unexplained rashes

Physical symptoms can be vague and may be the same as those caused by medical conditions so it is important to discuss them with your doctor. Many of the symptoms mentioned here could result without having added stress, but often stress is involved.

When our body prepares for battle, its focus is on our trunk area. The need for power and agility makes us think less and "do" more. Those same life-saving responses that we use for battle can also suppress our immune, digestive, and reproductive systems causing them to stop working normally.

Stress weakens the immune system and has been linked to medical conditions such as high blood pressure, heart attacks, and depression.

Our caveman Zugg experienced muscle tension as his body tightened up for battle. Pain in his low back, shoulders, stomach and chest may have been from muscle spasms. These spasms may also have been from fatigue from overexertion.

Suzie thought about the mornings she didn't want to go to work. She often felt butterflies in her stomach and pounding of her heart. She realized her sleeping patterns had changed and nights before work were often more restless.

STRESS AWARENESS

Your lifestyle and temperament play a contributing role in how you react to the stress in your life. To effectively manage stressors in your life, you must first identify them.

We all have daily biological cycles. Tuning in to them helps you pinpoint the times of day when your stress is greatest.

Do you find you have morning stress or late afternoon/early evening stress? If you know what time during the day you are prone to more stress, you can take measures to counteract it. For example, if you know early morning mishaps and commotions make you more stressed, look for a job that begins later in the day.

Suzie began to see her stressful times were mostly late afternoon. She woke with energy and enthusiasm, but as the day wore on, it declined. Many times, it was when she had skipped lunch or when she was trying to meet a deadline before day's end.

In addition to the time of day, someone's personality may play a role in how they respond to stressful situations. What's stressful to one person may be "all in a day's work" for another. The difference appears to lie in each person's perceptions of these various events. Mental health professionals believe personality plays a significant role in how we perceive stress.

There are two primarily different of personality types Type A and Type B.

People with "Type A" personalities are often rushed, ambitious, time-conscious and driven. They often feel they will never "catch up" and often try to save time by multi-tasking. You may recognize a type A person by their talking on the phone, reading the paper, and watching television, all at the same time. They are usually the driver that weaves in and out of lanes to save time when driving.

People defined as Type A personalities will always try to win. The stress of being the first one to reach the finish line, or be the winner of a game they are playing, is important to Type A people. Their body and mind are constantly charged and they are ready to battle.

When shopping, type A people are the one convinced the person in front of them in the express lane has too many items. They get impatient when someone wants to pay with a check or utilize coupons. Type A's are vulnerable to having a stress attack on the spot with no warning.

In contrast, the "Type B" personality is a much more relaxed, less time-conscious and driven person. Type B personalities tend to be less stress-prone because they are able to view things more adaptively. They are better able to put things into perspective, and think through how they are going to deal with situations.

Everyone has their own set of stressors. It is important to get to know what your stressors are before you can deal with them. A great way to begin managing the stress in your life is to make a list of the stressors you are facing at the moment.

External stressors are things that happen to you. They can be positive or negative and every human being experiences them. Examples of external stressors includes environmental stressors such as temperature, noise, or behaviors of people around you.

Both positive and negative family stressors can be external stressors. Getting a raise or losing a job can become an external stress. Workplace stressors can be from crowded personal space like having to share a desk or computer. If the parking lot is too small, not well lit, or is too far to walk, you may become stressed.

Having a heavy workload, getting additional responsibilities or conflicts with co-workers can also cause stress. External stress can stem from social events, friends, or community involvement.

Many of the stressors felt by Suzie were external. The temperature of her worksite and the noise level there resulted in chronic stress.

Caring for her children, her husband, and her elderly mother all contributed to external family stressors. Feeling unable to change the situation or to take a break from them resulted in Suzie feeling depressed and hopeless. It made her feel stressed.

Internal stressors, unlike external stressors are the things we think, or believe, or fear. Any thoughts or feelings, whether real or perceived, which generate anxiety or stress for you are often internal ones.

Whether you are having external or internal stressors, neither is better than the other. The goal is to define them and create coping skills to reduce them from filling your mind and body with stress.

Worrying about financial concerns or uncertainty in your life may produce stress as you struggle to find workable solutions. Even when we know our thoughts are surrounding irrational fears, we can become stressed by them.

Zugg became fearful and worried about his own death by a wild animal too. Although this thinking was irrational and only happened once in the numerous times he went hunting, these internal thoughts caused him stress. In Zugg's mind, he believed it could happen. This change in his belief system resulted in his not wanting to take a chance on being eaten, and reduced his desire to hunt.

What causes you internal and external stress?

ARE YOU STRESSED? A SELF-QUIZ

- Do you frequently neglect your diet?

- Do blow up easily and often?

- Do you frequently try to do everything yourself?

- Do you frequently seek unrealistic goals?

- Do you fail to see the humor in situations others find funny?

- Do you frequently and easily get irritated?

- Do you frequently seem to make a "big deal" of everything?

- Do you frequently complain that you are disorganized?

- Do you tend to keep everything inside?

- Do you frequently think there is only one right way to do something?

- Do you frequently get angry when kept waiting?

- Do you often get too little rest?

- Do you have few supportive relationships?

- Do you frequently neglect exercise?

- Do you frequently put things off until later?

- Do you often fail to build relaxation into every day?

- Do you frequently find yourself spending a lot of time complaining?

- Do you often ignore stress symptoms?

- Do you often find yourself racing through the day?

- Do you often feel unable to cope with all you have to do?

Add up the questions you answered "yes" to.   Your score today is = _____

Scores of 1-6 - Few Hassles   Scores of 7-12 - Pretty Good Control

Scores of 13-17 - Danger Zone. Watch out! Scores of 18+ - You are Stressed Out.

WHEN STRESS FOLLOWS YOU HOME

There is a saying, "A man's home is his castle." What happens when your solitude and comfort is overthrown by stress?

When we engage in relationships with others, be it family or friends, there is often love, passion, and respect. This relationship can also be filled with conflict and arguments as it isn't always easy to relate to each other. This love/hate seesaw is how we learn to bond and to learn about one another. It's giving in, compromising, and standing up for what you believe. It's how we develop as people and as a family.

The stressful situations felt in a family can be serious ones such as when faced with an unexpected illness or more minor as when a child gets bad grades. In the home, the stress might result in arguments about finances or even arguments over whose turn it is for trash duty. it's inevitable that each family will face stress together.

Families who are prepared for these trying times can emerge stronger and more prepared for future problems.

What stresses do you have at home?

Can we learn to leave that stress at the door?

"The greatest weapon against stress is our ability to choose one thought over another."

William James

Suzie was raising four boys and working outside the home, as well as caring for her live-in mother. Many of those years when the children were not at school she was only working part-time, but even those times were still not stress-free.

During the years of juggling work, parenting, and housework Suzie often came home tired and stressed. She was spent from her job and did not have it inside herself to pretend she was doing fine.

Maybe she did a good job of keeping a happy face at work, but when she came home, and her family asked me how her day went, sometimes, she exploded and although it was not their fault, the family felt it.

Tired and just wanting a sounding board and someone to listen to her, she inadvertently took her stress out on the family and was doing harm without realizing it.

Suzie knew deep inside that she was just one of millions of caregivers who cared for their family, someone with an illness, injury, or disability, and worked outside the home. She admitted having her mother living with her was at time fun and rewarding. Having been cared for by her mother when she was a child, it feels good to be able to care for mom now. Spending time together, telling old stories and laughing at pictures of when Suzie was young made them both laughs.

When Suzie went to her doctor, Dr. Moore for her yearly check-up, she shared her concerns with him. Her doctor listened to her story about caring for her mom and feeling overwhelmed and gave her a caregiver booklet to read. He asked her what were some of the additional tasks she had taken on with her mom living with her? Suzie said she helps mom by shopping for her, preparing and helping her eat food, and cleaning.

It is her responsibility to see that she is taking her medicine, bathing, and dressing properly. Her mother doesn't like to be left home alone and Suzie feels the need to provide her with companionship and emotional support.

Suzie admitted tearfully; she was angry that she no longer felt like she has any free time for herself.

Her doctor said, "it can be hard for you to juggle the different parts of your new life." A new life that now includes work, chores, caring for a family, and caring for someone who is sick. But he also reminded her that self-care was one of the most important things you can do as a caregiver.

Dr Moore assured her that having stress from being a caregiver is common, and most women and some men, are at risk for the harmful health effects of caregiver stress including depression or anxiety. Caregiver stress is due to the emotional and physical strains of caregiving. Many caregivers who bring their loved one into their home, are providing help or are "on call" almost all day. This often means there is little time for work or other family members or seeing friends.

Not knowing beforehand, many caregivers find they feel overwhelmed by the amount of care their aging, sick or disabled family member needs. This feeling of being overwhelmed can turn into guilt and stress to the caregiver. It's normal for you to have many different feelings about your role as a caregiver. At times, you may feel scared, sad, lonely, or unappreciated. You may feel angry and frustrated. You may feel guilty or feel that life isn't fair, and you may feel stressed. All of these feelings are normal for someone providing care to a loved one.

Women who are caregivers are more likely than men to develop symptoms of anxiety and depression. These symptoms can also raise your risk for other health problems, such as heart disease and stroke. Stressed caregivers may have weaker immune systems than non-caregivers due to lack of sleep and proper nutrition and may spend more time sick with the cold or flu.

A weak immune system can also make vaccines such as flu shots less effective. Also, it may take longer to recover from surgery. Just as in work-place stress, caregiver stress when combined with depression, can raise your risk for health problems, such as heart disease, cancer, diabetes, or arthritis.

What were some of the things Suzie could have done to reduce her emotional homecoming?

She could have learned to pause and do some deep breathing or listen to some calming music in the car before walking through the door. She would then walk in feeling more relaxed and be in a better mood before seeing her partner and children and mother.

Working women, homemakers and caregivers alike often tell themselves they can do all the household chores themselves. But to work outside the home, care for the family and still take care of themselves, is unrealistic. We must realize we do not have a super hero cape hanging in our closet. We must believe that it is alright to ask others for help.

To help reduce stress at home, sit down with your spouse and children and talk about the chores. No one enjoys doing household chores, but there are things that have to be done. Evenly dividing chores based on ability and age such as sweeping, taking out the trash, vacuuming, washing the dog, and raking the yard prevents potential conflict and added stress.

Asking for help not only reduces stress, but can be seen as a teaching moment with younger children. In doing so, they may learn not to become frustrated when they aren't fully capable of completing a task. Asking for help is an important life lesson many forget and, in the process of asking, the children will learn skills to help them live on their own.

Raising children who had soccer, friends, and homework had them scattered much of the time. One of the important priorities was eating dinner together, this was a special time for Suzie's family. Studies have shown that dinner hour is one of the most important. times in a family's life.

A study from Brigham Young University found that those adults who sit down to a family meal in the evening reported their jobs to be more satisfying and healthier, and suggests dinner together itself can reduce stress.

Taking time for communication and relationship building following dinner has benefits too. In doing this it can prevent future potential stressful problems to arise and to teach everyone how to respond to the pressures they are facing now.

Some stress can be good for you, it can help you cope and respond to a change or challenge in your life. Long-term stress of any kind, including work related and caregiver stress, can lead to serious health problems. Remember that you need to take care of yourself to be able to care for your loved one.

Learn some ways to manage caregiver stress and find resources.

When Suzie left the doctor's office, her head was spinning. When she reached home, while her mother slept, she read her pamphlet about ways to make caregiving easier and to reduce her stress.

•	Learn to tell whether your feelings are normal, or are signs of too much stress. If you are feeling overwhelmed and stressed, there are things you can do.

•	Talk to your loved one and your family. Talking about the illness and how you feel can help relieve stress. Talk with your loved one, other family members, or friends who can provide support.

•	Educate yourself about your loved one's medical condition. Find out all you can about the condition your loved one has, the treatment he or she is going through, and its side effects. Being informed can give you a sense of control. Your loved one's doctor, support groups, the internet, and libraries are good resources for more information.

•	Stay organized. Caregiving is often a full-time job. You may be doing it on top of other responsibilities. These could include a paid job or taking care of your children. Make a schedule with your family. This will help all of you stay organized and will help you manage the demands on your time. Don't forget to schedule time for things you enjoy. These could include visiting with friends, or going out to dinner or a movie.

•   Look for help in your community. Community services provide meal delivery, transportation, and legal or financial counseling. They also may include home health care services such as physical therapy, nursing, or respite care for Suzie. Respite care workers can stay with your loved one while you take a break. You can ask for help from support organizations or join an online community.

•   Joining a support group allows you to share your feelings and experiences with other people who are going through similar situations.

Before she had left his office, her doctor shared that recognizing that you need help takes strength and courage. It can be beneficial to talk with a counselor. He then referred her to a therapist who specializes in caregiver and work stress counseling and encouraged her to talk about

Forgive me for the times, even now,
when I question your judgment.

As I go about the many daily tasks of
caregiving, give me energy.

As I watch my loved one oh-so-slowly
walk across the room, give me strength.

As I answer his/her repeated question

just one more time, give me patience.

As I look for solutions to whatever

Signs of on the job stress

The classic symptoms of job burnout include doubt of one's capabilities, decrease in job satisfaction, increased absenteeism and lowered efficiency at work. While you may not be on the verge of job burnout, you probably are one of the growing majority of Americans who report that their job causes them stress.

A 1985 study conducted by The Center for Disease Control and Prevention's National Center for the Health Statistics found that more than half of the workers surveyed experienced moderate to severe stress in their job.

If not addressed and managed, job stress accounts for an incredible amount of personal misery for employees and cost companies billions of dollars.

Of course, we know that every job includes some difficulties in which the worker is expected to adjust and accept. These job difficulties alone do not cause burnouts, more often it is the workers lack of control over his job situation that leads to uncertainty, frustration and eventually burn out

Chronic stress comes from situations where your stress response is triggered again and again without giving you a chance to relax and recuperate between each episode.

One of the primary sources of chronic stress is stress from your job. When job stress turns chronic, it can threaten our physical and emotional health in several ways. The responses to stress when we, like Zugg, are under attack or facing real danger can be beneficial. They are not beneficial however, when we are dealing with continued pressures and threats at work like Suzie experiences.

Suzie found a quiz on an internet website that showed her what her work stressors were and what to do about it.

Three steps to begin to manage job stress.

1 identify your symptoms of job stress.

2 identify the sources of your job stress.

3 identify how you can better respond to your specific job stresses.

Suzie listed her symptoms of job stress including brain confusion, frustration, and in addition to the finger tapping, she developed headaches and "butterflies in her belly."

What were her top three sources of job stress? Lack of control over getting important information, generation gap conflict with supervisors who were younger than she was, and environmental stress from going over the bridge that always seemed to have a morning accident.

How did Suzie respond to her specific job stresses?

Suzie realized the lack of control she felt caused her to become annoyed. In her mind, those "young bosses" picked employees who were closer to their age for special projects. This resulted in her feeling angry and frustrated that her advancement was conceivably stunted by the date of her birth.

Sitting on the bridge waiting for another accident to clear was sure to bring on that finger tapping and her being frustrated.

Situations that are causing you stress such as too little time to complete tasks, poor leadership, and overly competitive colleagues who may not work as a team, are just a few of the reasons that cause constant stress at work.

When we're stressed to the max, we often don't take time for our family or friends, having fun time or even sleeping.

Believing that you can get by on just a few hours' sleep is only a delusion. If we don't get eight hours of sleep on most nights everything suffers. Our physical health, emotional health, our well-being cognition and even conceivably decision-making may be compromised.

This lack of sleep and pushing on at work, can possibly lead to depression or anxiety or worse.

In the world of today, we accept that we're going to have some stress. But added work stress often makes things worse. As our normal stress constantly simmers, new, added stress from tensions at work, can leave us in a constant state of worry and frustration.

What can Suzie do about all of her stress?

• Set goals to help her respond more effectively to her job stress. Change the response to external stressors by taking regular breaks as you are able to. Getting up and moving around or to step outside for a few minutes can do wonders to re-center you after feeling stressed. Keep a sweater at the office for when it's cold.

• "Turn off" the job when she leaves work by shutting the work cell phone off and not going on the computer.

• Three internal changes she can make include learning to find balance between physical exercise and being relaxed. Eat properly, rather than fast-food and vending machine snacks instead of taking a more nutritional lunch break. Making sure she gets sufficient sleep so she is mentally prepared for those never-ending stresses.

• When you set goals be specific and break them down into small bites, write them down and re-evaluate them every once in a while, to see if they need modification.

• Making positive changes may be beneficial, but it's not always easy. Reward yourself when you achieve a goal by creating awards for every goal that you establish. Maybe you'll buy the book that you wanted to read and set aside time to enjoy it.

When you have a controlling boss, it feels as if your freedom, your success, your finances and your family are all at risk. Perceived or real threats to our values, our self-images, and our job performance can all trigger chronic stress.

When we are in the middle of this stressful situation, our emotional well-being can push us into a sacrifice syndrome. Our bodies or mind can't keep up with the threats and don't work as well as they should, and emotionally, we are a wreck.

One goal to aim for is to be able to talk with your boss about what is expected of you, how you are doing in your current role and what happens if something goes wrong.

This is often scary because we feel if we disagree with our boss, our job may be in jeopardy. When not in conflict, learn ways to negotiate with your boss.

It's important not to just rant and complain. This gets you nowhere. Instead, be able to present your position and negotiate with them. State the problem, state how you feel about the problem, state how that's affecting your productivity, and offer a win-win solution that you have.

Given all this information, some workers still continue to try harder, give more of themselves and become even more stressed. They often do this by working unreasonably long hours and not taking those required breaks. At home, they answer work emails and take calls about work at night and on weekends.

Studies have shown that American workers are likely to skip their vacations more than any other country's workers. Why?

Some say it is because they are worried what will happen at work while they are gone. Others are believing this display of loyalty and availability to your company will secure their position. Doing this may, in fact, produce the opposite results when they develop burnout.

When our bodies and minds are worn down, we tend to become pessimistic and may get frustrated more easily. Our judgement is not as sharp and our interactions with co-workers may suffer. If all this happens as a result of increased work stress, why do we continue to behave this way?

Because many of us are in denial about the impact of increased stress in our lives.

Work Site Stressors Checklist

Rate each of the ten stressors listed below on a scale of one to ten, one for low impact and ten for those that cause a high impact stress to you.

I have unfavorable relationships at work such as:

- Distant coworkers or supervisors

- Aggressive colleagues or customers

- Clashing relationship with boss

- Incompatibility with boss or coworker

I have little say in the decision-making process, including:

- Responsibility without much authority

- To voice my opinions or feelings, jeopardizing my job

- Not being included in important planning meetings/decisions

- My decisions are often challenged or contradicted or ignored

My job conflicts with social/family obligations because of

- Incompatible working hours with family needs

- Constant shift changes

- Change in working hours

- Transfer to a new office/location

Unpleasant or unsafe work environment or commute such as:

- Negative change in working conditions such as a decrease in privacy

- Long commute with lots of traffic

- Noisy or hazardous environment

- Uncomfortable environment: poor lighting, recycled air, no windows

- Physical discomfort: long hours sitting or standing

There are uncomfortable aspects about my workload such as:

- Deadline pressures

- Information overload

- Decrease in hours and! or income

- Too much or too little work

I am hassled or discriminated against at work due to:

- Sex, color, or age

- Religion, politics, or fashion

- Appearance, life style, or values

I don't feel adequately appreciated for the work I do because:

- Inadequate pay for amount of work

- Others take credit for my ideas

- Boss is highly critical and rarely says thanks

- There is little or no opportunity for advancement

I do not have job security because of:

- Recession-related business reorganization- lay-offs, mergers,

- Bankruptcy

- Ambiguity of job description

- My over-qualification or under-qualification for the job I hold.

- Highly competitive and shrinking job market

My job, or my job description, has changed or is changing due to:

- Promotion

- Demotion

- Retirement

- Change to a different line of work

I do not feel proud or rewarded by my work because:

- It is tedious and treated as trivial at work

- It isn't the type of work I want to do or isn't my field of interest

- There are conflicts with my values and beliefs

- My friends/family don't respect what I do

The purpose of quiz is to assess what stresses you out the most at work.　　Your __ Total Score

Job Stress Score Rating: 10-29 Low 30-59 Moderate 60-80 High 81-100 Intense

INTERRPRETING YOUR RESULTS and CHOOSING YOUR BATTLES

o   Review the list and categorize the stressors according to those you can change and those you cannot change.

o   Focus your time and creativity on those stressors you can change. (for examples) What is your contribution to a difficult relationship with your boss or co-worker? Do you need to learn to be more assertive regarding deadline pressures or unpaid overtime work?

o   Are some of the stressors ones that you cannot realistically change? (for examples) A long commute with lots of traffic, incompatible working hours with your spouse, or a hazardous work environment?

o   Acknowledge those stressors you cannot do anything about and "let go" or reconcile yourself with this lack of control. This is a challenging task, and perhaps a life-long project. Start small in learning to let go of those things you have no control over.

"The greatest mistake you can make in life is to be continually fearing you will make one."

– Elbert Hubbard

The Stress of Working

Eighty percent of all workers feel stress on the job, nearly half say they need help in learning how to manage stress and 42% say their co-workers need help, too.

Inward symptoms from stress such as depression and self-doubt are not surprising. Outward behaviors such as having apathy at work caused by stress have also begun to arise.

14% of working respondents felt like striking a coworker in the past year, but didn't. 25% have felt like screaming or shouting out loud because of job stress.

Over half of all surveyed said they often spend 12-hour days on work related duties and frequently skip lunch because of stress from job demands.

Workers who have higher levels of job stress experience a greater incidence of the common cold, and call in sick more often. There has also been a documented link between high job stress and increased risk of mental health issues, such as depression or anxiety disorders.

Some of the on the job stressors experienced by Suzie, myself and other workers interviewed resulted from a perceived lack of control or lack of organization. Poor working conditions or environment sets the foundation for a job to be successful or a struggle.

Suzie mentioned she had personality clashes and felt alienation with her co-workers.

•   When a co-worker, your boss, or even you have unrealistic expectations of the job, it can lead to stress, frustration, being overworked, and a decrease in one's sense of accomplishment.

•   Working with uncertainty of your job, whether fear of job loss, possible merger or downsizing can make an employee stressed.

•   Sometimes we accept a job that is not a good fit for several reasons. Maybe it was the need for an income, a job close to an employee's home who doesn't have a car, or doing something you don't enjoy can result in stress.

• Feeling like you are not adequately trained, informed, or not given a clear job description can result in stress.

• Inequality and gender-related bias continue to exist in many workforces of today.

When real or perceived opportunities are halted due to one's race, lifestyle or upbringing, work ethics and inspiration may become diminished.

When not given the opportunity to grow and rise in a company, the job may become unchallenging and the goal of excelling declined.

What are some ways you are stress at work?

In a perfect world, everyone would have a manageable case or workload and know and set boundaries and limits. We would not be afraid to use as many "others" as possible in completing our work and to work as a team.

Like me, many others are afraid to say they are overwhelmed with their caseload or to ask for help from others, seeing this as a defect or risk to their job security.

The reality is that letting your boss know you are overextended and could use some help is good for the whole company. Working together for the betterment of the company builds relationships and creates a positive environment.

When needed, take a mental health day. Find time to laugh, joke, and have time to unwind. Learn to take a holistic approach to taking care of yourself – mind, body, and feelings.

Encourage your human resource department to offer materials, workshops and training seminars related to job stress.

Lastly, get your work and home life organized. Having said that, don't stress about the need to be perfect or having everything in place immediately. Everyone can start with baby steps.

Feeling out of control in a situation is why many people become stressed. Often the things we are worried about, are in fact, out of our control. When you begin feeling anxious ask yourself what you can do about this situation.

We have no control over what other people think, their thoughts and how they feel. You can try your best to influence them and make them change their way of thinking, but in the end, they will make up their own mind.

Once we begin to understand we can't make everyone like us, and that is ok, we will become less stressed. One of things we don't have control over, that can cause us stress, is our past. As humans we often cling to thoughts, people, and even items that seem to identify who we are. Fearing that if we get rid of them, we will cease to be us.

Are you still angry over a previous relationship that ended? Are you still holding a grudge because something did not go your way? Are you a "people-pleaser" who tries to make everyone around you happy? Remember that we have no control over other people's thoughts, feeling and actions, simply "Let it go."

Taking control of your own life doesn't mean taking extended breaks or not completing required tasks at work. It means taking control of what you can. Your health, finances, relationships, and some work situations. It means being responsible for your own behavior and feelings, but understanding you don't have control over other's behavior or feelings.

You do have the control to teach or influence others with your actions.

I used to say if I could have a super-power, I would want control over people's behavior and be able to get other people to do what I wanted. This was evident as I silently wished my sons, as young children would clean their rooms and treat each other nicer.

Every person has control over their own
behavior and the choices they make.

Watching my boys grow up, go to school, get jobs, and plan to marry, I had little control over their success. How I raised them and, with what values may have helped, but it would be up to them to become successful in their future. We can hope for honesty from others, but we have no control over it.

You may say" That's quite a list, what do I actually have control over?"

Control

Just like we have tried to influence others, people may try to influence us as well. In the end, we are in control of our own happiness and our health. Although we may be inflicted with an illness, how we chose to fight or accept that illness is something we have control over.

We have control over the quality of our lives and our attitudes.

A woman I met was diagnosed with cancer. She chose to have treatment and did what the doctor suggested to fight and regain that quality of life she once had. This was a difficult road for her to take, but she actively listened to others who helped her build a new way of life.

Being strong enough to ask for help and assistance is something we have control over. Our attitudes in life, the thoughts we have, and the things we say and do are all within our control.

Setting a goal to open your mind to new ideas and being non-judgmental or critical and accepting others actions may be a positive step when you find yourself in a situation that you have no control over.

When faced with one of those situations you cannot control, you have two options: Learn to accept what you have no control over, or change other circumstances in your life that can help you cope better with these situations.

We do not have control over others, but we can offer assistance and be sympathetic to their needs.

Once Suzie was able to develop coping skills for reducing her stress, she began to see she was not the only employee stressed. When she noticed a coworker was feeling stressed, she gently approached them. She shared her story and told them she noticed their stress, and would like to help.

Listening and being empathetic to their issues, she offered to help them by focusing on one problem at a time. Letting them know she would be available when they need to vent and to take an extra break or two if needed.

Taking a quick walk together outside during their lunch break gave them both a mental as well as physical pause from all the work responsibilities. Sometimes, it is as simple as sharing a smile and laugh together. A simple smile or a good laugh can reduce stress significantly and quickly. If you have a positive attitude, it will spread to others and can help them cope with their stress.

Excessive stress can often be prevented by revisiting why you are working in your current position. Do you enjoy what you are doing? When you enjoy what you're doing and stop worrying about what others think, you are on the path to managing your stress.

Be confident, but realistic to your expectations and limitations. When you need support and guidance, don't be afraid to ask for help. If you do make a mistake, be gentle with yourself and let yourself off the hook.

Don't keep focusing on that issue when you make a mistake. Instead, remember nobody is perfect and think about all the things you do well.

Reducing stress begins by having a well-rounded life, one that is not always focused on work. How much of your time each week is spent on each of these areas?

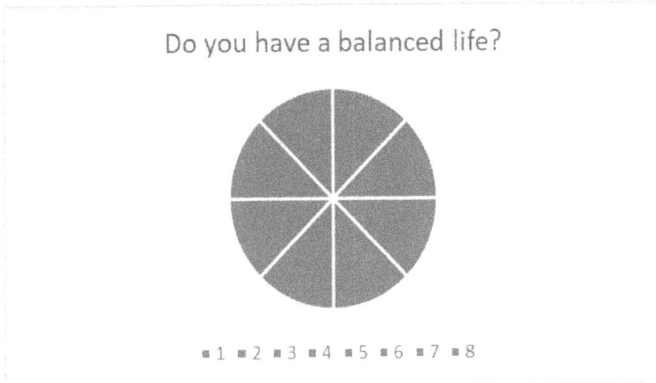

Do you have a balanced life?

■1 ■2 ■3 ■4 ■5 ■6 ■7 ■8

How do I spend my time each day?

Self-Care -   Work   - Intimate Partner/Family - Friends/Social Life   - Financial - Spiritual Aspects Health & Wellness/Body Image -Community/Service

Using a scale from zero to ten, rate your satisfaction with all eight sections.

Do you spend more than the average of 1/3 of your day on work related tasks? Do you want to find more of a balance?

Job stress is a widely inescapable problem, and has been found to affect people from all industries, and income levels.

Did the numbers surprise you? Are you satisfied with the ratio? Do you spend more than the average of 1/3 of your day on work related tasks? Do you want to find more of a balance in your life?

Because job stress is a leading cause of chronic stress, managing factors we experience on the job can cut out significant levels of anxiety and lead to greater wellness and happiness.

One way to reduce job stress is to learn techniques to smooth your transition from work to home.

Developing a transition from your work world into your home and family world is not often seen as a form of self-care, but ignoring this process can result in added stress and cause one to become burned out.

Mentally and physically leaving the tasks behind that we have been immersed in for the 8-12 hours can often be very difficult and challenging. But if incorporated into one's life can be beneficial.

Brandt's Story

Brandt, a man who works the 3rd shift has created his own transition rituals. Before heading home, he often meets his wife and they have breakfast together. Talking about his night, their life and goals as well as listening to her share stories of her day.

Most of us who work at a "9-5" job follow a ritual before we go to work: morning coffee, walk the dog, drop the kids off at school, read the newspaper. Due to his working hours, he does these things after work and utilizes them to unwind and transition into a husband and father.

Creating a ritual for the end of your work day, one that disconnects you from work is just as important as our rituals that transition us unto work mode. Whatever type of transportation you use to go from work to home, use that time to do something that clearly shifts you to a different place and mindset.

• Set limits- We carry very high expectations of what can be accomplished in 24 hours and try to achieve "one more thing" at work before we leave. This way of thinking can turn an 8-hour day into a 9- or 10-hour day, one that cuts into our personal time.

• Balancing the "must do's" - (laundry, dishes, car upkeep) with the "want to dos" (read a book, go to a concert). Negotiation with oneself and family, so that the less enjoyable activities still get done and there is still room for the fun activities.

•

Make a monthly calendar with a schedule for yourself and everyone in your household to avoid the stress of last-minute craziness.

If after trying these suggestions and you still have job stress, maybe it is time to change jobs. Knowing when to quit after making a genuine effort to modify your own thinking, behaviors, and work conditions can be freeing. Sometimes you may find that your job is still dissatisfying, not suited for you.

Ask yourself whether the price you are paying cognitively, emotionally and physically is worth the material benefits. If the answer is no, consider a career change. If the answer is yes, look at the ways to manage your stress in the future.

"

Reducing Stress

Have you ever wondered how some people are able to handle extremely hectic schedules and still seem calm and relaxed? One reason is because they have effectively learned to manage their stress. We all know that stress can cause us to perform at work poorly resulting in less productivity.

When we have too much on our plate, we have trouble concentrating and may not accomplish the things we planned for the day. The added stress only escalates the problem.

As Suzie began doing research at the library and on the internet, she learned there are stress-reducing activities that utilize the brain, the body, and even help with behaviors that cause us to be stressed. She found several stress-reducing practices she currently enjoyed and some she would like to try.

She had discovered there may be just as many ways to de-stress as there are things to make one feel stressful. She smiled to herself as she found some funny, and even strange suggestions on ways to reduce stress.

One article suggested you pop a sheet of packing bubbles or bubble wrap. When she read that all she could imagine was the stress of those around her every time one of the   bubbles would make a loud "pop".

She laughed out loud when she read on an internet site from Prague about a spa where they offered beer infused hot tub sessions. The spa was claiming the hops cultivated a mixture of vitamin B and that they use special hops from the Zatec region. Of course, they did serve pints of beer to you as you soaked in the hot tub. This leaves one to wonder if it is the beer outside your body or the beer inside that was relaxing you?

Armed with all the information she had gathered, she prepared herself to create a self-healing regime.

The process for her, involved developing a stress-reducing plan suited just for her. A stress-reduction plan generally involves learning some coping skills for when stress arises.

The plan also stated that she should be doing something else, something she felt was more productive. The reading material said the best thing we can do for others, is to take care of ourselves.

Some activities might be exercising, practicing breathing techniques, or engaging in creative activities, such as singing or creating art. It may also include eliminating or reducing sources of stress in your life, such as excessive cell phone or computer screen time.

Take a look at your own activities, are there some of them you no longer enjoy or don't have time for?

Writing down an actual plan for reducing your stress makes it more likely you'll carry them out.

•   Sweeping your negative feelings under a rug will not make them go away. Acknowledge and accept how you feel, but begin to look at what is causing those feelings and take action to change unwanted feelings.

•   When something upsetting happens, and chronic stress begins building up in your life, sometimes simply talking about it with someone who can listen nonjudgmentally can be the first step to you feeling a more calming effect.

•   Make time for fun and play. Everyone needs to recharge from time to time by doing things they enjoy.

• Having fun is a natural stress reliever. When you are having fun, you are right there in the present moment. Enjoying what is in the here and now.

• Think of the last time you had fun, when you played and laughed. You didn't worry, there was no tension or anxiety. Do that again, go and have fun. Lots of fun.

• Laugh much and laugh often. Laughter is a powerful stress relief tool. A 10-second belly laugh equals 10 minutes on a rowing machine in the raising of one's heart rate (exercise reduces stress).

As mentioned before, the brain cannot distinguish between when stress is real or is a re-thought at a later time, the same is true with laughing.

There was a study at Stanford University once where they divided the participants into three groups. The first group were entertained by comedians and shown cartoons. They laugh and smiled during the show. When they measured their vitals before and after, they found a decline in their vital scores.

The second group, a control group was placed in a room with no stimulation. The vital scores before and after did not change at all. Interestingly, the third group was told to just laugh without stimulation. When checked, their vital scores had decline just as the group laughing from the cartoons.

Sometimes, if I really just need to unwind and
kind of watch something that isn't gonna stress
me out or have drama in it, I watch 'Spongebob.'
Kelsea Ballerini

When a follow-up visit was completed, both groups, one and three reported less illness, less hypertension, and over all better health than group two.

As with this study, it is a scientific fact that the body cannot differentiate between real and fake laughter. The benefits are the same.

Laughter is also known to increase feelings of well-being, increase your creativity and lower blood pressure. Laughter reduces one's cortisol levels and stimulates the production of endorphins.

When your body comes under stress or experiences pain neurochemicals called endorphins are produced in the brain's hypothalamus and pituitary gland., Endorphins, can also help bring about feelings of euphoria and general well-being.

Watch your favorite comedy movie or television show. Netflix and Hulu give us a massive selection at the press of a button. Laughing over a bowl of popcorn with a friend is a positive way to reduce stress and put a smile on your face.

Chewing gum has also been reported to not only freshen your breath and reduce snacking, but can also reduce anxiety and depression. In a 2008 study conducted by Andrew Scholey, Ph.D., participants who regularly chewed gum demonstrated lower levels of anxiety, increased alertness, reduced stress and improvement with multi-tasking.

Chewing gum actually lowers your cortisol levels, the hormone responsible for stress. But chewing gum doesn't just reduce stress, it also makes you more alert and improves your performance in memory-oriented tasks. It does so by increasing the blood flow to your brain and alerting your senses.

Travis Bradberry

Swear No, swearing at the person you're mad at might not be the best idea. But even if the object of your frustration isn't around, swearing has been shown to be great stress relief. In Germany, there's even a hotline you can call to swear at trained operators whose whole job is to get you as angry at them as possible! Sadly, a similar hotline doesn't exist in America.

Take photos Stop scrolling through your Instagram feed and take some photos of your own instead. Photography literally helps you gain a different perspective on the world, which keeps your own stress in check. Make a conscious effort to find positive photos – looking for the good in the world will reduce your stress levels.

Jen's Story

Stressed out! This is a term that I believe is overused. However, I truly am always stressed out and anxious. I have that classic "Type A" personality. Always moving, always worrying, and never ever feeling good enough. I am a perfectionist and I like things to be organized. Yet, live in a chaotic and ever-changing world.

As a result, I am continually trying to regain some semblance of control. My life is a whirlwind that moves way too fast. Like most people, I have too much to do and not enough time, and too many responsibilities with insufficient resources. I find myself holding my breath and clenching my jaw consistently throughout the day and night. I literally am "Tied up in Knots!"

Currently, I am a single Mom of two busy teenagers. I work two jobs and am maintaining and hanging onto my home by a thread. Did I mention I also have a dog, a cat, a bunny and a bearded dragon to care for? I love my life, my kids, my home and my little zoo.

I am grateful. However, I joke (but it's really not a joke) that I need at least three clones: one to work and pay bills, another to drive my kids around to all of their various commitments and appointments, and one to do the yardwork, cleaning, laundry and other ubiquitous household chores.

Then, the real me could eat, sleep, and relax a little. Maybe then, I could be the person I want to be. I could spend quality time with people, not feeling harried or guilty for being so inadequate all of the time.

I have supportive friends and family that help make all things possible for me and I have terrific kids. Yet, I somehow always end up feeling alone. I feel like everyone is always mad at me. Unfortunately, I end up always being mad at myself.

I have been asked how I manage stress and reduce anxiety. My immediate answer is that I don't! However, once I dug deep and really gave it some thought, I realized I have the perfect answer: Photography.

I was reminded of a documentary I saw years ago about September 11th and the attacks on the World Trade Center in New York. What stuck in my memory were the words of several photographers and reactions to their part in documenting the tragedy.

I did a Google search and found a few quotes. One said his lens acted as a filter: "The things are happening over there, on the other side. Another quote that imprinted me and I'll never forget: "I let the camera absorb all the disaster or the sadness of an event. It protects ME from the event."

Do not misunderstand. I am in no way trying to compare my stress or my life to that horrific event. It simply resonated with me that if these people could use their cameras as a shield, so can anyone and for any situation.

My thoughts are this is a legitimate way to handle the stuff that stresses you out, big stuff and small stuff!

I love taking photos. There is really nothing I would rather do. I need a bumper sticker; "My other car is a camera!" or "I'd rather be snapshotting!"

Not too long ago, I gained an awareness that is difficult to explain. When my camera is around my neck or I am looking through the lens, I think of absolutely nothing else except my subject. All of my worries disappear at least for those few moments, or sometimes hours.

This is even true at parties or in social situations. Instead of being anxious about meeting people, or remembering names, I use my camera as an excuse or as a shield. It is the ultimate conversation starter and invisibility cloak at the same time!

So perfect! I have never been the type of person who can meditate. I lack time and patience. This feeling of being "in the zone" is the closest I get to mindfulness. I strongly connect to that well-known quote about a woman's mind being a browser with 2,857 tabs open all of the time. When I take pictures, the internet is down and nothing can distract me.

Photography allows me to freeze time and slow down. Photography gives me confidence and a feeling of being in control. Most importantly, my photos generate a sense of purpose and unexplainable focus that I correlate to meditation. The result: My pictures are a gift I share with the world around me. They are a present I bestow upon myself.

It all started when I was in high school. Like so many others, I never felt as if I belonged. I struggled and did not enjoy school.

Everyone seemed so fake to me. Even though I had good grades and I was smart, I still had trouble getting out of bed in the morning. I was discouraged and bored which led to a serious lack of motivation.

One year, I was fortunate to find Photography on my schedule as an elective. This is back before smart phones and digital cameras and all of the editing applications available in today's technical age. We had a darkroom and developed film. My Mom let me borrow her old Minolta. This was so exciting to me and afforded a much-needed outlet to focus on something other than my mundane routine. I had a reason to attend class. I'd like to say I moved on to become a famous, award winning photographer, but that is not the case. In fact, it's only in retrospect that I realize how much it helped me get through that time.

Only now I can look back and say that was the true beginning of the benefits of photography in my life.

My children's inheritance is in the hall closet. Hundreds, no, probably more like thousands of pictures all labeled and chronologically sorted into beautiful books. Back when my daughter was a baby and I was pregnant with my son, the decision was made that I would become a Stay at Home Mom. Even with a college degree and a good job at a big company, the costs of daycare were overwhelming. To make matters clearer, I cried all the way to work after I dropped my daughter off at daycare every day. I knew she was in good hands. I simply missed her. I knew it would be the same for my son once he was born.

My husband at the time was in the military and we were relocated to a small town in North Carolina which amplified the need for me to be at home.

I worked part time but I focused mainly on my family and raising my kids. I documented all of the milestones and moments with a simple and inexpensive Nikon digital camera I purchased at Wal-Mart. I snapped pictures of first steps, first meals, and every birthday. I have photos of the zoo, the beach, the park and all of their childhood friends.

This was so much fun to me.

Kids grow up so fast. It's not just a saying. One day you are changing diapers and the next you are taking them to obtain a Driver's Permit! By taking all of these photos, I was able to freeze any particular moment in time!

My camera forced me to stop and focus instead of thinking and worrying about every little thing (as most Moms do!) I stayed up late at night to hook up my camera to the computer with a cable and transfer the files.

I vividly remember taking the time to have them printed and sit on the floor with photographs all spread out so I could place them into the albums carefully. I adored the process. It provided me confidence and a sense of control over my world. I was purposeful and focused instead of worried or tired or stressed. That closet of photo albums is my treasure map to my children. It is a precious gift to me that I am extremely proud of.

Eventually we were transferred back to my hometown in Florida. Smart phones had been around for a few years but I always resisted due to budgetary reasons. I finally acquiesced and also joined Facebook at the urging of friends and family. My Nikon went by the wayside and was replaced by my phone camera.

What a gift to have easy access and portability! My kids were getting older but that didn't stop me from continuing to annoy them (a Mom's ultimate job) with my incessant picture taking. At the same time, I began experimenting with beach and sunset photos. The sand, water and fresh air had always been a source of peace and joy for me.

In North Carolina, the coast was about an hour drive. Here in Florida, I am lucky enough to be just minutes away. The beach and my pictures became an escape for me. Unfortunately, my marriage was coming

and tensions were high in my home.   Night after night, I would manage stress and anxiety by slowing down, and freezing time with beautiful, colorful images. This started to resonate with my Facebook friends and family.

The positive feedback I received had an effect to my core. I actually believed that maybe, just maybe, I was actually pretty good at something. I was good enough. In hindsight, I think my motivation and purpose in taking and posting these images was my attempt to make people happy.   In turn, to receive positive feedback and bring myself some comfort and happiness!

A few years ago, I received my first REAL camera as a Christmas gift! A Canon DSLR (which I now know stands for Digital Single-Lens Reflex.)   I cried. I actually cried tears of absolute joy. This camera has built in Wi-Fi and I am able to transfer images directly to my smart phone anywhere and anytime. This sure is a long way from my high school days with my Mom's old Minolta and canisters of film!

I continue to take photos of my kids, although now they are less cooperative as teenagers. Beach sunsets are my specialty.

I even had an opportunity to photograph a wedding for some dear friends. It was one of the greatest accomplishments and honors of my entire life. My experiments and education far from over as I delve into a new world of digital and editing.

> Photography is a great way of handling and managing stress and anxiety. It is one vehicle I use to untie those knots in my life that I just can't handle sometimes

I am not a professional photographer. Nowhere near so. Not yet but maybe someday. In the meantime, you can find me enjoying every second behind the lens!

In closing, anyone can take pictures. No need for a special camera or expensive equipment to reap the benefits. Chances are you already have the perfect tool in your pocket. Here are my tips, and a few tricks. First, if taking photos of your kids, don't worry about the messy or unpleasant times. Go with it! Some of my favorite photos are the kids crying over their birthday cake! This holds true for pets and family get-together too! Second, watch your background for unnecessary or distracting people or objects. Sometimes you just need to make the tiniest adjustment to capture a better shot., everyone knows!

Don't think, just go take a picture! You just might loosen up those knots. You are worth it!

> To reduce stress, give yourself permission to
> be a kid again by getting in touch with your
> inner child. Jen

Scream Think screaming doesn't sound fun? Think again! When you feel like you're about to explode, screaming is a cathartic and secretly exhilarating way to release all your frustrations. Drive to a secluded spot or just scream into your pillow. You'll be surprised how much better you feel. Just make sure to warn any loved ones if they happen to be nearby.

Break something Just like screaming, shattering an object is a fun, cathartic way to reduce stress. Just make sure it's an object you don't want or need. And make sure you break it in a way that keeps everybody safe. You may need to find an isolated area or get some safety goggles. And be sure to wear close-toed shoes!

Jump in the water While there's no one but you in the water, it is a great way to reduce stress. An ocean dip works best and immersing yourself totally is recommended, but a lake, stream or pond would also work. Don't live near a body of water? Try a pool or even a relaxing bubble bath.

Play with bubble wrap Bubble wrap is a pliable transparent plastic material used for packing fragile items. Regularly spaced, protruding air-filled hemispheres provide cushioning for fragile items. en.wikipedia.org Everybody loves popping bubbles on bubble wrap, no matter how old they are. And in fact, it's been proven to reduce stress! Just make sure you do it for at least a minute for best effects.

Ever wonder why children are never that stressed? Maybe because they have playtime and then they get a "time out" at nap time. It's pretty easy to give yourself playtime as an adult. Play tag, fly a kite, get some Play-Doh and make something or build with Legos.

Our body reacts to stress in five areas. Each area has its own way of reacting to and managing stress.

Physical

Getting your body moving can reduce stress. Endorphins are released as we exercise, walk, jog or even swim. Pick your own physical way to reduce stress. My neighbor has two daughters who swim at our condo pool several times a week. When they swim, they set a goal of fifty laps! Watching them, I found myself feeling inadequate when completing less than ten laps. Swimming was actually stressing me out. Learning they had been swimming this way their whole life and I had just started a routine allowed me to not beat myself up, but to be grateful I was able to complete my own laps.

Having someone to exercise with can be fun, but again, remember what kind of exercises are best for you and don't allow someone else to choose the activities for you.

There is a saying that "Variety is the spice of life" Don't stick to a routine that is no longer fun or does not meet your needs. Select another way to manage your stress.

Emotional   Common belief used to be that if we didn't express every emotion we felt (or at least the big ones), they would show themselves in other ways. Distracting oneself from emotional pain with emotionally healthy alternatives — such as a feel-good movie, fun activities with friends, or a satisfying mental challenge — can lessen emotional pain and help us feel better.

Social   The stress of a conflicted relationship can take a heavy toll on your health and well-being. Relationships that are sometimes supportive yet, sometimes unpredictably conflict-ridden can be particularly difficult. Maybe it is because there's an underlying sense of uncertainty and tension.

Cognitive Our ability to focus, concentrate and remember has a lot to do with how much emotional stress we are experiencing. Emotional stress has a major impact on our immediate and long-term cognitive functions, and underlies many of the mental health problems in society today.

Spiritual I have been told that the impact of a religious commitment helps reduce stress both physically and mentally has been demonstrated to be overwhelmingly positive. The religiously committed person is generally more satisfied with life and marriage. Possibly, regular time spent in prayer or just being part of a non-judgmental community is its own stress reducer.

> "Spiritually minded people are often mentally and physically healthier, live longer, are less stressed, and are less likely to commit suicide or abuse drugs."

The stress of a conflicted relationship can take a heavy toll on your health and well-being. Relationships that are sometimes supportive yet, sometimes unpredictably conflict-riddled can be particularly difficult because there's an underlying sense of uncertainty and tension. Because of this, it is very important not only to know when to let go of a toxic relationship but to know how to keep all the relationships in your life healthy.

When we are angry, frustrated, anxious, depressed or feel other negative emotions frequently, and for long periods, it is likely we are experiencing unhealthy levels of stress, which adversely affect heart coherence.

Social media for many is a stress reliever. Scrolling through the internet mindlessly reading posts and taking fun but useless quizzes. Facebook and other websites for many others, are a stress builder. Comparing oneself to the happy pictures of places others go and families where everyone is always smiling fills them with envy, guilt, and stress to improve their own lives.

Studies have shown people often only post a happy picture of themselves and have struggles and stress just like all of us do. Counselors have suggested people fighting stress take a vacation from the media sites to reduce their anxiety.

Curious about how my friends reduced stress while not on social media I went to Facebook

- Mary Anne - listens to relaxing music, take nature walks, yoga, meditate, watch the sunset.

- Dale - Work out

- Linda - Walk, write, take photos!

- Tirena - power walk

- Mark -Range time and nature time.

- Marina -Work out at Curves!

- Michelle - I have effectively changed the way I think about things and thereby greatly reducing my stress levels.

- Michelle- Cuddle my puppy

- Ron -exercise or music or just some deep breaths.

- Laurel ¬- Go on Facebook

- Brandt- Sing Karaoke, baby!! Toastmasters. I hate to admit it, but sometimes I relieve stress by cussing.

- Robin ¬ Eat. play computer games. housework. Exercise. Walk. Working out is a great stress reliever.

- Joy - Pray

- Julie -Run while I listen to an audiobook! in a stressful moment when I need a quick fix to calm myself, I do deep breathing.

- Amber - Meditate!! I use it every night to stop my wandering mind. Essential Oils!!!!

- Michaele - sing, bake really rich, homemade brownies, and watch Stardust. Snuggle my cats.

- Kathy - I get away and if i can't I play mindless games and when possible, I play the flute.

- Susan -Don't watch the news

- Richard -Head to the woods or water!

- Kathy -Yoga. Journal

- Vicki - Love on a cat

  Deborah - Play my flute.

- Renee -Take a long walk with some awesome music

- Dale - I write novels, so I get to escape to strange and new places I create.

- Alice - Certainly not go on Facebook. LOL. I read a good book or go on a walk or bake bread.

- Cathye - Call my friend Mary Jane

Some of my friends in the Facebook survey spoke about resting their minds and bodies. When I was younger, I was taught resting was for lazy people and it was discouraged.

"Rest is not idleness, and to lie sometimes on the grass under the trees on a summer's day, listening to the murmur of water, or watching the clouds float across the sky, is by no means a waste of time." John Lubbock

Using our Brain to Release Stress

The good news is that we do not have to remain stressed. There are ways to train your brain to handle the stress and increase your productivity and get more joy in your life.

> "The greatest weapon against stress is our ability to choose one thought over another."
> » William James

There are safe, natural and free ways to train the brain to release 'feel-good' hormones to help stay relaxed and calm. The most obvious is by engaging in relaxing activities. These exercises help wire the brain to be calm and relaxed as opposed to the normal day to day demands that may stress us out.

When threats are overestimated in our minds, we find ourselves worrying too much and causing us more stress. A great tool to manage stress is to remember a time when you felt strong and could cope with just about anything that was thrown at you. The brain is only able to focus on one thing at a time, thinking of calmer, happier times will result in lowered stress. Deep Breathing is a conscious focused way of getting your body back to a normal rhythm.

Deep Breathing Have you ever had someone tell you to take a deep breath when you are feeling overwhelmed or upset? Although you may think they are being silly, this may actually be a good thing.

Breathing may seem to be something we do automatically, but many of us do it wrong. Shallow breathing is what many of us do normally and even when faced with a stressful situation. Improper breathing, rather than calming us down, makes us anxious. We are not inhaling the needed oxygen or releasing carbon dioxide.

Breathing exercises have been proven to reduce anxiety, depression, muscles tension, even headaches. Breathing in deeply may seem unnatural at first, but once you feel the actual benefits, you will be more conscious of the way you breathe within your day-to-day life.

If this practice seems a little un-natural at first, close your eyes and put your right hand on your abdomen and your left on the center of your chest.

Which hand rises the most when you inhale?

If the right hand rises more you are breathing with your diaphragm and this is the correct way to breath. If, however, your chest rises more, you are breathing from your chest and not getting the full benefit of the breath.

To begin to learn deep breathing, inhale and let all the air out, such as when you blow out candles on a birthday cake. Do this a few times to push all the air from the bottom of your lungs.

When you begin your next breath, be mindful of making your abdomen rise.

When practicing deep breathing, focus on a calmer state of mind as you distract yourself from overwhelming thoughts and sensations. Sit in a quiet area and practice the following: Take a slow, deep breath through your nose, allowing both your abdomen and chest to rise. Once your abdomen is fully expanded, breathe out through your mouth, just as slowly as when you were breathing in.

This type of breathing has helped me when in a traffic jam on a bridge. Feeling out of control to go either forward or backward, my heart and pulse begins to race. By practicing what I call the 3-6-9 breathing technique, I am able to remain calmer until the cars start moving again.

THE THREE—SIX-- NINE PLAN

Exhale completely through your mouth, making a whoosh sound.

1.   Close your mouth and inhale quietly through your nose to a count of three.

2.   Hold your breath for a count of six.

3.   Exhale completely through your mouth, making a whoosh sound to a count of nine.

This is one breath. Now inhale again and repeat the cycle three more times for a total of four breaths.

Exhaling takes three times as long as inhaling. The ratio of 3:6:9 is important.

Once you develop this technique by practicing it daily, it will be a useful tool that you will always have with you. Use it whenever anything upsetting happens—before you react. Use it whenever you feel internal tension or stress. You can even use it to help fall asleep.

Suzie tried doing this exercise. As predicted, she had been breathing incorrectly to get the most air. She was a bit skeptical that this would do anything for her stress, but she found she was wrong.

After doing the 3—6--9 breathing she found was feeling calmer. She was a bit light headed, but read that was normal the first few times because we are not use to breathing this much oxygen.

Music has been shown throughout scientific literature to be beneficial for a broad range of health issues, including Alzheimer's disease or dementia and depression. When it comes to negative emotions, music can uplift most individuals' spirits or relax their mind, because music can influence our brainwaves.

Your brainwaves are what help you relax and increase your ability to fall asleep. Researchers at Stanford University have confirmed music is a great relaxation tool based on its effects, as well as its availability. Musical preference varies widely between individuals, so only you can decide what you like and what is going to help you reduce your stress. Calming music before bedtime promotes peace and relaxation and helps to induce sleep.

When people are extremely stressed, there is a tendency to avoid listening to music. Have you ever turned the car radio off when you were lost or feeling stressed?

Singing (or shouting) along to your favorite songs can be a great release of tension. Karaoke is very enjoyable for some extroverts, but would add stress to others! Find out what works best for you.

There have been several studies that prove the benefit of music to reduce stress. Listening to music with headphones has been shown to reduce stress and anxiety in hospital patients. Listening to music can relieve anxiety and depression while increasing self-esteem in elderly people.

Music choices can vary from person to person. When Suzie wants to unwind, she may listen to music of her teenage years or if she wants to relax may play instrumental music. Listening to music that produces a happy memory, such as what was played in your younger days can aid in reducing stress.

Reduce the stress levels in your life through relaxation techniques like meditation, deep breathing, and exercise. You'll look and feel way better for it Susan Somers

Meditation is the practice of focusing your attention on one thing at a time. This item can be a tangible item such as a candle's flame, a flower, or a single word or item from your past. The main goal is to condition your mind to only think of one thing.

Our minds don't normally do this.

Think about when you are trying to go to sleep and your mind wanders to events, action, and people. Research has shown meditation just before going to bed can improve mental and emotional health and reduce thoughts of prolonged stress. Not only does meditating teach individuals how to gain greater control over their body and mind, but it also promotes mindfulness.

What is mindfulness?

Mindfulness is said to be the basic human ability to be fully present, aware of where we are and what we're doing. It is having the ability to not be overly reactive or overwhelmed by what's going on around us.

When individuals become more mindful of their thoughts, they are better able to identify and recognize unhealthy thought patterns and realize what it is causing them to feel stressed. Mindfulness encourages the person to live in the moment, instead of stressing about the past or future.

Rather than lying down to relax, as with the breathing exercises, mediation is often done upright. Begin by sitting in a chair with your knees apart and your hands at your side or crossed-legged on the floor.

Sitting upright, straighten your back and let the weight of your head relax. Find the position you feel most comfortable in by rocking back and forth and side to side.

As with the breathing exercise, become aware of your breathing. The goal is to keep a passive attitude but realize, as a beginner, you may have many thoughts and difficulty with concentration.

You may only be able to remain still for five minutes or so when you begin. With practice you should be able to do this for twenty minutes or so.

Suzie's suddenly remembered her first experience with meditation was when she was in college. The professor had everyone sit in their chairs, close their eyes and try to let our mind rest. It was very hard for her to do. She did struggle to remain still for the five minutes and had a hard time keeping her eyes closed.

Suzie felt she had "failed" mediation. With a laugh, the professor explained was even though she did not feel she was relaxing, did she feel any different when she opened her eyes? Did the colors around seem brighter? Did her breathing change? The benefits can happen even though you don't think they have.

Meditation simply allow your mind to release and relax. Approach this with a pleasant attitude, a spark of playfulness, and good humor.

[Cite your source here.]

Go to a quiet place where you will be free from distractions for fifteen to twenty minutes. Loosen clothing. Remove glasses/contacts and shoes if you wish. Sit quietly and comfortably. Place both feet flat on the floor. Use the back of the chair to support your whole back so that your spine is comfortably erect. This frees the diaphragm and disinhibits energy flow through the spinal column. Think of a bamboo pole that goes from your head to the base of your spine. Two holes at the top and bottom release all the tension from your body.

When meditating, your chin is neither up nor down, but is resting comfortably, perhaps slightly back to straighten the neck. Rest your hands in your lap. The shoulders, neck, and chest are very relaxed.

Gently close your eyes, if that is comfortable. (If not, keep them open at half-mast, looking at a spot in front of you on the floor.) Relax your entire body. Start at your feet and relax each part in turn. Especially relax your abdomen for deeper breathing. Let your facial muscles be smooth and relaxed in a pleasant, peaceful expression. Breathe gently and peacefully through your nose. Take regular, rhythmic, slow, abdominal breaths.

Become aware of the gentle coolness of the air going into your body and the pleasant, relaxing feeling as it leaves. As you concentrate on breathing, allow external stimuli to fade into the background.

Much like when we are walking away from the beach and the sound of the waves begin to fade into the distance until you barely notice them Let the sounds of the world around you gently fade until you hardly notice them as well. Notice that the simple act of breathing is pleasant. Just be aware of your breathing and enjoy its pleasant rhythm.

In closing your eyes and paying attention, your breathing tends to slow down and become more regular on its own. Don't try to make this happen, just notice whatever the breath does this.

Imagine the breath to be like gentle waves on the shore. Ride the waves of the in-breath as you inhale. Ride the waves of the out-breath as you exhale.

Should distracting thoughts or worries enter your mind, just greet them cordially and without judgment ("That's OK; that's life.") Watch them float and disappear into awareness. Continue quietly and peacefully for the next few moments. Let the word "one" fill your awareness, reverberating peacefully in your mind. Eventually you, your breathing, and the word "one" become one.

End your meditation rather slowly, allowing the peaceful feelings to spread to the rest of your body and your life. If you are interested in learning more about meditation, there are many books and videos available that will offer additional meditation exercises.

Guided imagery is another relaxation technique that helps the brain reduce stress. This example encourages the use of one's imagination to picture something or someone that makes them feel relaxed. Perhaps you went on a beach holiday with family, and it was a time of great pleasure and relaxation.

Our minds are creative when it comes to our imagination. If we think unhappy thoughts, we will become sad. If we think anxious thoughts, we will become tense. To reduce the unpleasant or unwanted thoughts, we need to refocus our mind to positive, healing thoughts. There is a saying "The power of positive thinking," and guided imagery is a perfect example.

When you focus on imagery, utilizing all senses, you create a powerful and relaxing experience.

Although some people are skeptical, numerous studies have confirmed the association between imagery and positive health.

Guided Imagery can help your physical and emotional stress. Many times, stress from events prior, during, or even in the future can cause physical strains. Finding a calm place within yourself can be beneficial when your emotions get too difficult to face.

The mind can only focus on one thing at a time, and if you focus on a positive memory the anxiety felt may begin to subside.

To practice guided imagery, Suzie got into a relaxed position and closed her eyes. She began by visualizing all of her muscles starting to relax.

Using her deep breathing skills allow her to drift to a semi-conscious stage. Letting her mind drift to a place in her past where she felt happy and safe.

With her eyes closed, she imagined a special place from her childhood. For others, it might be a room, a house, a field, or even a tree fort. Any place that brings a smile to your heart.

Suzie thought of her grandmother's house. It made her smile as she thought of the living room that had a child sized rocking chair that she always sat in. She could almost smell the cookies grams always made and the softness of her apron.

When you practice guided imagery pay attention to what it makes you think of. Use your five senses to make the place come to life. What do you see? What does it smell like? Do you hear any familiar sounds?

When you have opened your eyes and returned to the present, think about your adventure. Guided imagery is like going on a mini-vacation without leaving your chair. Practice this whenever you feel overwhelmed or stressed.

Suzie thought about her evenings, when the day had ended and she was retiring for the night, there were times her mind did not want to shut down. Thoughts of the day and concerns about tomorrow filled her head.

By using guided imagery, she was able to drift to sleep. she visualized herself sleeping in various settings. Sometimes she was on the beach, or in a hammock with the breezes gently rocking her to sleep. Other times, she envisaged she was sleeping in her own bed and dreaming positive thoughts. Doing this often brought her the desire sleep and she awoke more rested.

The Power of the Beach and what it does to your brain to reduce stress is amazing.

Take your seat on the shore. Listen to the ancient voice in the waves. Taste the salt of life on your tongue. Run your fingers through the eternal sand. Breathe deeply. If you find yourself worrying about your cell phone and emails, if you find yourself feeling guilty that you should be doing "something important," breathe deeply again. And again. Breathe deeply until every fabric of your being is reminded that this, being here, is your top priority. This is peace. This is wisdom. The work, is a means to living, but this is the living. Brian Vaszily

Suzie liked the sounds of that quote. She admitted she didn't take time for herself much anymore. The job, kids, and her parent's needs left little time for what she called "self-indulgence".

Thinking back to her younger days, she thought of her mother. During the cold and often stress-filled days of winter in New Jersey, her mother would wistfully say" I'm going to retire in Florida and live by the beach". We all smiled and nodded approvingly, never thinking it would become a reality.

Prior to her fall and the need for more care, she remained in New Jersey. She visited often, but had never moved to Florida permanently. Suzie and her sister followed her dream and both had lived in the Tampa Bay area for several years. Many people's minds drift to Walk Disney World and Cape Canaveral with thinking of Florida, but Suzie's mind drifts to the beach.

Growing up on the Jersey shore she had beaches in her bloodstreams since birth. As a child, she had eagerly awaited Memorial Day when it was "acceptable" to go into ocean. She smiled thinking of her teenager years, going with friends to Wildwood. Piling into someone's care, they would find the perfect spot and put a blanket down on the warm sand near the water's edge. Just sitting there, her problems seemed to drift away with the tides.

Research have discovered that spending time by the ocean is good for your wellbeing.

Data published in the journal "Health Place" stated that those who live by the coast report better physical and mental health than those who don't. If you are lucky enough to live in homes with ocean views you may be feeling calmer than those without that view.

Maybe this is one of the reasons Hawaii has earned the ranking of being the happiest state in the U.S. by the annual Gallup poll six times since 2008.

As humans, our moods and behaviors are affected by color. The color blue has been found by an overwhelming amount of people to be associated with feelings of calm and peace. Gazing into the ocean can actually change our brain wave frequency and puts us into a mild meditative state.

Our sense of smell is one of our most powerful senses and is often used to reduce stress. The smell of the ocean breeze can even contribute to your soothed state.

This may have something to do with the negative ions in the air that you're breathing in at the beach.

Finally, the sense of touch contributes to the feeling of relaxation. The simple act of touching the sand or of putting your feet in warm sand causes many people to relax.

Although those living with an ocean view report feeling calmer, you don't have to live by the water to reap the benefits. It's all about taking advantage of the time you spend there, no matter how brief, by practicing mindfulness.

To benefit the most from your beach experience, leave technology at home or in the car. Sit still, close your eyes and listen to the ocean waves rolling in and out. Don't let distractions take you from this peaceful moment.

Above all, be aware of your senses. "Focus on how your body feels warm from the rays of the sun. Pay attention to what your mind is telling you as you place your feet in the sand and wiggle your toes. Take deep breaths to allow you to smell the ocean air. The stress of the day will melt away and you will feel more relaxed.

Stephannie's Story

As I search for my flip flops, my toes are like Mexican jumping beans. My heart starts beating with an overwhelming calm kind of excitement. As I grab my beach bag and keys, there is a full-blown tingle all over my body. I arrive at the beach, take my flip flops off, and as soon as my toes touch the sand, calm...pure and utter calm.

I take a deep breath in of that amazing salt air as I allow it to cleanse my lungs and soul. I set up my spot and sit down. All of a sudden, I look out and see the most beautiful sight nature can bring.

This is the perspective I have waited to see. I breath in again, listening to the waves crash and allow them to take away my anxiety and stress. How can this be?

For me, the beach is the purest form of calm and power.

When I come to the beach, I can put my mind at rest. I can think about what is triggering or causing my stress and anxiety. I grab my notebook, which is always in my beach bag, and just start writing.

Doing this keeps me out of the vortex of spinning out of control. Sitting at the beach, whether for ten minutes or for hours helps me manage those difficult situations. It helps me find clarity and perspective in my life.

The ritual of getting ready and having those moments are precious to me. By taking something, I love to do, without even knowing it, I turn it into the most amazing healing process I could have ever imagined.

Although I have other coping skills, when I am going through a rough time in my life, I find I am drawn to the beach and my perspective and clarity begin to change.

Using our Bodies to Release Stress

When you take the time to cleanse your physical body of accumulated stress and toxicity, you are rewarded with increased vitality and optimal health.

Debbie Ford shares these words "Contrary to relaxing the brain by sitting still, using the body to release stress often involves moving. Becoming more physically active is beneficial for one's overall health as it promotes both mental and physical well-being."

"Those who think they have not time for bodily exercise will sooner or later have to find time for illness." – Edward Stanley

Studies have shown exercise can reduce mental fatigue, improving concentration and focus.

Exercise activities include brisk walking, jogging, yoga, and even heading to the gym and using traditional equipment.

Exercising improves circulation and lowers blood pressure. It also helps clear one's mind of worrying thoughts and anxieties.

Robin's story

Growing up, my mother enrolled me in dance lessons because I was a clumsy and awkward child. I wasn't a natural dancer, but I enjoyed it. The music, the precise movements, the discipline it takes to perform well in ballet, tap and jazz kept me in training until I was 47 years old. I loved going to class a couple times a week. It was my escape from life and my chance to focus on myself even as I raised two children.

Once I stopped dancing, I did nothing. My body aged. My mind aged. Following a divorce, the weight and the depression crept in. Going through these difficult personal times and suddenly becoming a single mother, I was prescribed antidepressant medication to help me cope. It was a stressful time.

From time to time, I joined a gym, but I never stuck with it. Working out on machines didn't connect with me like dance did. There were also times when alcohol would be my stress reliever. Never at inappropriate times, but more often than it should have been.

I was depressed, stressed out and didn't like who I'd become: overweight, disinterested and relying on a glass of wine as a pick-me-up. I would sit on the couch each morning and think about how I should get up and exercise, but I did nothing. I was locked into a self-defeating cycle.

About five years ago, a friend invited me to go to the local YMCA with her. I also needed to lose 20-30 pounds; so, on my first visit I did a circuit on the machines. The draw for me, though, was that there were so many classes to choose from! I wanted to get back in the game and feel good about myself.

The next week I was huffing and puffing through a low-impact aerobics class. I struggled to keep up with the women in their 70s and 80s in the same class, but I hung in there. The music and movement brought me back to life.

After a month of dance and water aerobics, I was disappointed in the weight loss. I met with a personal trainer who gently patted my hand and reminded me that "at my age" I wasn't going to lose weight doing aerobics.

He recommended weight training and told me about some new training classes developed by New Zealand Olympian Les Mills

One of the most popular classes is Body Pump, a high-repetition weight-lifting session focusing on each major muscle group.

I was intimidated! But I had made friends with Mary, a woman in my aerobics class who was well into her 70s. She took Body Pump every week after aerobics class. Not to be outdone, I joined her. I loved the music. I loved the challenge of pushing my body.

I consistently participated in two classes a week. It took me about a year to lose 19 pounds and drop one pant size. I felt stronger, leaner, and more confident about myself. Approaching the age of retirement, I had way too much time on my hands which raises my anxiety. While I was going to the gym three times a week, I had nothing to do on Saturdays so I ventured into another Les Mills class – Body Combat.

Again, I loved the music and the class environment. Body Combat utilizes high-energy mixed martial arts-inspired workout that is totally non-contact. Like in dance class, I was once again mirroring the instructors to form the proper moves. While I can't do all of the jumps that the 30-somethings can, I find that the punch and strike combinations help me clear my head and body of all the stress and anxiety accumulated through the week.

I was one of the oldest people in the class, but I didn't care. Once again, I was focusing on me and my needs. I was having fun moving to the music.

Several months ago, I made a long-distance move. It was a huge disappointment to learn that none of the gyms in my new location held Les Mills classes.

The move was fraught with problems and without my usually gym schedule to help me work through things, my anxiety and my stress level increased to a near breaking point.

The stress weighed heavily on me. I wasn't a fun person to be with.

Once I settled in my new home, I discovered Les Mills on Demand. I now have a workout studio in my basement where I can stream Les Mills classes on a TV. I'm back in the game with about four classes a week and feeling much better about myself.

I'm not done yet with new challenges. This winter I plan to take snowboarding lessons. If I have to live where it's cold, I might as well find something fun to do. At 66 years old, exercising to music and pushing myself beyond my physical limitations has helped me feel physically fit and mentally at peace. I'm happier and enjoying being back in the game.

After reading Robin's story, Suzie was beginning to feel discouraged. She had never been good at sports or physical activities. Her mind drifted back to her middle school years, she remembered always being picked last for games at recess. She wasn't the only one to see she was not athletic.

Determined to find a physical way to reduce her stress, she discovered the benefits of her local community pool. Whether it was with a group of others doing water aerobics or swimming alone, she discovered she felt better afterwards and even slept better.

Pet Therapy is also a physical way of taking your mind off of your stress. According to PubMed, owning a pet can increase a person's health in many arenas. Studies have shown that dog owners are much less stressed than those who do not own a dog. One thought is in receiving unconditional love from an animal that love you, can play a big part in making their owners happy and less stressed.

Spending time with a dog, even if it's not your own, can beat stress. Animal assisted therapy has been shown to provide powerful stress-busting benefits like easing anxiety and depression and lowering blood pressure, according to several studies.

Although cats and dogs are both a primary pet choice and both can be stress reducing, dogs have been shown to be especially good at de-stressing humans. One reason for this may be because beginning thousands of years ago, dogs have been bred to be a good companion by responding to our feelings and human emotions.

The hospice where I worked brought "hospice trained" dogs to visit patients in their care centers. The patients always seemed to smile a bit more after the visits.

Heather's Story

Dogs are incredibly versatile creatures, and it turns out that man's best friend can also be a surprisingly good life coach. Three months ago, I adopted a 3-year-old Plott Hound mix named Carter from the Humane Society.

I had never heard of Plott Hounds, but after a quick google search I learned that they are the state dog of North Carolina; a medium sized powerhouse of a dog, bred for hunting bears.

As you can imagine, a dog intended to run free in the woods, tracking and wrestling bears is a little bit out of place confined to my one-bedroom apartment.

I do the best that I can to meet his activity needs though. We go for miles of walks every single day, with a little jogging reluctantly mixed in to let him stretch his legs.

We play tug of war, he gets food puzzles, bones to chew, and as many outings as I can manage throughout the week. Carter is a very high energy dog, but he's also incredibly sweet. When we aren't exploring the great outdoors or playing together, he loves to cuddle with me on the couch and tries to curl up in my lap - all 55 pounds of him.

This new exercise partner, this new companion, has also turned out to be a surprising source of life wisdom. In our three short months together, I've already learned about the merits of practice, finding joy in life, and overcoming difficulties. The concept of practice is something we learn at a very early age.

We practice all sorts of skills in school, and hopefully continue on as we grow through adulthood. It's not that Carter has taught me how to practice, rather he has reminded me of how important and powerful practice really is. We enrolled in a 6-week dog obedience course. We learned a new command every session, and our homework was to practice that new skill for 7 days so we could build on it with something new the following week.

It's hard to know how the start of the course would have gone for Carter, because it was I who failed miserably that first week. We didn't practice at all, and Carter didn't learn a thing. I learned my lesson though, and we practiced all of his commands every day for the rest of his course.

After 6 weeks I was shocked by how much he had learned with only a few minutes of practice every day. He knew sit, stay, lay down, drop it, leave it, watch me, and wait.

Seeing Carter's success has reminded me how important it is to actively work towards the personal goals I have set for myself. Even though life is busy, it's important to find moments wherever we can to practice. Making a regular effort is essential. Otherwise we will get to the end of the week, or the month, or the year, and find that nothing has changed.

The most fun lesson I've learned from Carter is to experience joy in the little things every day. Carter is so excited about life; every morning he can't wait to start the new day.

I can barely get out of bed without him pouncing on me because I'm not moving fast enough. But there's just so many awesome things waiting for him.

Awesome things like a walk outside! And the squirrels! And breakfast! And playing! And burying his toy in the couch! And more squirrels! And it happens every day! And every day it's still exciting.

That enthusiasm for life is contagious. I am finding myself excited to wake up and start a new day. Not quite for the same reasons; frankly, I could do without the 3-mile walk at 5 in the morning.

However, after our walk I am excited to come home and have my glorious first cup of coffee.

I find myself delighting in the small things all throughout my day. I pause when I see the sunset or the beautiful full moon. I take an extra few minutes to snuggle with Carter on the couch. I'm downright giddy when I put on my sweatpants after a long day. Those little enjoyments have helped bring balance back to my life. There's so much to stress over and worry about, but there's also a lot of fun and joy if we only take the opportunity to experience them.

Carter has also brought me a profound realization: we can overcome life's most difficult experiences.

Looking back, I have been through many situations that were overwhelming and seemingly hopeless. We all have. Anxiety, depression, addiction, losing loved ones... very heavy experiences, and when we're in the middle of them, it's hard to see the light at the end. And yet, I've gotten to witness how we can overcome those experiences, either personally or through someone close to me.

Carter has become a daily reminder of that inner strength we possess.

Up until two years ago, I had two dogs: Toby and Rufus. I had each of them from the time they were a tiny puppy, and they were the lights of my life. They were life companions and helped me through many transitions: through college, through a divorce, and through multiple moves including the very first time I moved out on my own.

I was devastated when I lost them both in 2017 less than 7 months apart. Toby was the first. He developed cancer in his old age and passed away at the age of 14. Rufus was a shock though. He was still fairly young at only 8 years old and in perfect health, but he collapsed very suddenly during a routine trip to the dog park and was gone in an instant.

I'm convinced he died of a broken heart because of how bonded he was with Toby.

That year and the year after were so difficult for me. I didn't think I would ever have another pet again. But after many months of grieving, processing my emotions, and reminiscing about the good times I had with my boys, I finally got to a place where I began to consider adding a new furball to my life. Now I have this awesome new adventure named Carter.

Practice, joy, and overcoming difficulty are just a few of the many lessons Carter has taught me in 3 short months. We've also covered patience, attitude, and social skills, and I'm certain there will be more throughout the years.

There's a bumper sticker out there with the slogan "who rescued who," and now that I have Carter that phrase has come to have personal meaning.

When I adopted Carter, it was to give him a good home and a better life, but he's had more of an impact on my own life than I ever expected. I may have taught him how to sit, stay, and leave it, but he teaches me invaluable life lessons, is a daily inspiration to be a better version of myself, and has pounced his way into my heart.

Relaxing your muscles involves movement of the body, but also utilizes the mind. Based on a two-step process it is suggested you start by taking fifteen minutes a day to practice this method. For those who are always stressed or experience persistent feelings of anxiety, this exercise can also help them recognize what it feels like to be relaxed.

The first step is to intentionally tense up specific muscles, such as the shoulder muscles. The next step is to release that tension, understanding how the muscles feel once they are relaxed. You can then use this relaxation technique to help reduce overall tension.

This process will also help you become more mindful of stressors. Walkers can even concentrate on relaxing their muscles as they walk.

Start by focusing on a particular muscle or muscle group—such as your shoulders, neck or jaw. Tense the muscles while you take a few steps as you walk, then slowly release the tension. As you do this, you'll feel the tightness begin slipping away.

Practicing muscle relaxation had proven to work well for Suzie. Before going to sleep, she would take about fifteen minutes and tighten and relax her muscles. With less pains from the day or muscle group she was able to get a more restful sleep.

Dancing is something we think we need to be good at to do. Turn on the music and dance like no one is watching. Forget about if you're any good and just let loose. Pick up your favorite CD and dance in your living room or bedroom. Dancing is a good physical exercise, and it releases those endorphins that make you feel better.

Read a book and go on an adventure through the pages. Losing yourself in a good book may be a surprisingly simple and low-tech way to beat stress. "Some people find great relief in reading.

Everyone knows that reading makes you smarter because it fills your brain with knowledge, builds a better memory, improves writing skills, and increases vocabulary. These are all positive reasons to read, but to discover that reading can also reduce our stress levels is even more exciting. There is documented scientific evidence that states people who read on a regular basis improved their perceived stress, anxiety, and quality of life.

According to the University of Sussex studies, reading for just six minutes has been shown to reduce stress by 68 percent.

Whether it something inspirational, a piece of great literature, or it may be something just reading can be fun. Read a joke book out loud alone or share them with your partner or friends and giggle together.

One her journey to discover stress reducing techniques Suzie had read several textbooks, but she had never sat in a comfortable chair and read for enjoyment. While at the library she found just the book to take her on an imaginary escapade without leaving that comfortable chair.

Checking out a copy of Swamp Archeologist (Dead End Kid Adventures Book 1) by D. W. "Dick" Powell, she soon was on a journey with eleven-year-old D.W. into the deep, dark swamp at the end of his road. Together Suzie and D.W would discover clues to a long-forgotten robbery gone bad.

Painting can be fun and also reduce stress. You don't have to be as talented as Vincent Van Gough to benefit from arts and crafts. Art and music therapy alike are proven methods often used to relieve stress. This is because the activity takes your mind off whatever it is that is stressing you and promotes relaxation.

Gathering in a group and painting has become popular in my community. Some events are offered as an evening class with alcoholic beverages, other events are open to all ages during the day. These are focused painting sessions with everyone painting the same picture as the instructor.

Remember finger painting as a child? Try doing it again. Craft stores offer kits and can be done alone or with a bunch of girlfriends. Try listening to your favorite music, get some non-toxic paints and a lot of paper and have fun. You can even finger paint with pudding- licking your fingers is the best part.

Suzie decided to put this suggestion to the test. She invited a few friends over, made some of her special white Sangria and put on some foot-tapping music.

Wearing a large men's shirt, she had bought from the thrift store, she placed the paper and paint pots on the table. Some of her friends were apprehensive about putting on their shirts and paint on their hands. Some of them even joked that Suzie was crazy. Once they all began "playing" and glided their hands into swirls of various colors, they were all soon laughing.

Connect with that playful kid in you and finger paint yourself. Enjoy the colors, the sensations, and the freedom of playing with your hands. Even after the activity, when they had all returned to their daily lives, they admitted they did so with less stress and a clearer mind.

Walk away your stress; There is a connection between walking and stress reduction.

Consider this scenario: You're at work and your boss tells you that you have to turn in that big report you have been working on for months, two weeks early. Your blood pressure surges. Your pulse races. You start feeling stressed. What are you going to do?

Rather than impulsively give the boss a piece of your mind, try going out for a stress-reducing, lunch-hour walk. Taking time out to pursue an activity like walking can get your mind off distressing concerns. Walking can also give you a feeling of detachment from daily pressures. With a chance to wander, you may be able to see the situation in a new light and come up with a solution to your situation.

There are several stress-busting approaches to walking. It can be regarded as a social activity, offering an opportunity to enjoy the company of friends or family. Conversely, it can also be done alone, allowing you the freedom to sort through your thoughts or listen to music. If you're stressed-out and plagued by negative and unproductive thoughts, try concentrating on your walking technique and your breathing. When you combine walking with taking long, deep breaths, your mind tends to become more aware and alert.

Walking has been reported to help you change your whole outlook -- easing the way for confidence and peace of mind to replace that stress, fear, depression, and anxiety.

We all need a constructive method of releasing physical energy and emotional stress. Exercise can provide that safety valve. In particular, walking can help relieve stress, thus improving your mood and mental outlook.

The NIMH (National Institute of Mental Health} panel on exercise and mental health concluded that exercise can help relieve muscle tension and reduce hormones that serve as messengers of stress. Exercise may also reduce stress-related emotions, including anxiety, anger, aggression, depression, and tension.

Renee's Story

As a stress reducer I can absolutely say that walking can definitely calm you down and get your stress level low. Power walking for at least 60 minutes a day can increase endorphins which produce a natural euphoria that gives a great feeling. For me personally, I prefer to start my day off with a good 4-5-mile walk. It's easy because all you need is comfortable clothes and shoes. Some people will listen to music or watch a program on their phone which makes the walk seem to go faster. Sometimes if I walk a little before bed and then take a shower, I sleep much better at night. I would definitely suggest a good walk next time you feel stressed.

Suzie met with a neighbor who took daily walks around the condo community. She sighed and said "I will never get up to walking 4-5 miles a day like Renee."

Her neighbor smiled and gently told her she didn't start out walking for thirty-minutes every day. Starting out slow she walked for five minutes, turned around and walked back home. She did these walks three times a day to build up to the recommended thirty minutes per day. A health coach had told her it didn't matter if you did it all at once, how far you walk, or even what time you walk. What mattered was that you start walking. Walking forces you to look at your surroundings, to focus on something other than being stressed. Suzie asked her neighbor if they could walk together sometime as she got use to adding activity into her life. With a grin, she said "I'll meet you here tomorrow and we will begin."

Massage was something Suzie once thought that people indulged in to have an enjoyable afternoon. Following a car accident, it was recommended she visit a chiropractor. Once adjusted by Dr. Erika Meister, a chiropractor in town, she suggested massage to relaxed her inflamed muscles. Following her first treatment by a licensed massage therapist, she began to understand the many benefits of massage when your body is stressed.

Not meant to be a one-time event, Suzie discovered there are tremendous benefits to be achieved through regular massage therapy treatments.

Whether your need is to have a moment of relaxation, reduce muscle tension or attain relief from chronic pain, a therapeutic massage can enhance your overall sense of emotional and physical well-being. Newsweek magazine published an article that when massaged regularly for ten days, premature babies gained 47% more weight and left the hospital six days earlier than those not receiving a massage.

Kerry's Story

Many studies have shown that massage relieves tension, reduces stress, relieves anxiety, improves sleep, helps digestive disorders, reduces headaches, and the list can go on and on.

One of the reasons it helps you relax is because you are feeling the tension in your muscles literally being ironed out during a massage. The tension seems to leave your body with each glide.

On a deeper level, when you get a full body massage, it actually improves the circulation of blood and lymphatic fluid, which is a clear fluid found outside the cells which cleanses the tissues. When trigger points or "knots" form in your muscles, they actually put a restriction on the blood flow, or in other words, the nutrients traveling throughout your body.

If you have a tight diaphragm from rounded shoulder posture. This really dampens not only the full drawing capacity of the lungs, but it also is robbing the body of a decent percentage of oxygen. The lack of adequate oxygen leads to shortness of breath, which leads to muscles being "anxious" because they don't have enough oxygen to energize and repair themselves.

The result of the muscles being anxious leads to chronic pains and injuries. These chronic pains and injuries eventually lead to one being an anxious mess that can't ever seem to relax.

A good massage should get deep enough to treat the trigger points in your muscles, but not so painful that you are jumping through a wall like a "looney-toon" character.

A massage therapist has to be able to get deep enough into the muscles that they release those trigger points that are preventing the blood flow from getting to where it needs to go, your whole body!

Massage therapy can be an important part of your health maintenance plan. Reducing stress within your body can help reduce the stress in your mind. Some of the benefits include reducing or eliminating pain, improving joint mobility, improving lymphatic drainage, and reducing muscular tension.

Essential oils scents are powerful -- a simple smell can immediately trigger a powerful memory, place, or person. Scents have power to evoke emotions and memories instantly and can directly impact our bodies through our nervous system.

Aromatherapy is a complementary and alternative medicine practice to massage that taps into the healing power of scents from essential oils extracted from plants.

Essential oils can be diluted by water, diffused into the air or a few drops can be gently rubbed into acupressure points on the body. One study found that lavender oil aromatherapy calmed the nervous system -- lowering blood pressure, heart rate, and skin temperature as well as changing brain waves to a more relaxed state.

Ashley's Story

Essential oils came into my life at a time where I felt I had nowhere else to turn to for help. I was in my third-year teaching, my mother became ill, and I just could never keep my head above water. I was introduced to essential oils by a fellow coworker and my first thought was "Wow, this smells amazing!" Never did I think that these oils held more benefits than just smelling great.

Through the support of my amazing team and many informational classes & resources, I have learned that essential oils not only offer physical benefits, but also emotional, spiritual, and mental benefits as well.

Essential oils are naturally occurring aromatic compounds found in plants such as trees, flowers, and seeds. These oils give the plants their smells and help to protect/repair the plant.

Stress affects everyone differently so I will outline the benefits of some of our most commonly used essential oils and you can decide what resonates with you. But before going into the types of oils, I feel it is important to discuss the ways essential oils can be used. First and most common way is to apply the oil topically to the affected area. Many oils can be applied directly to the skin "neatly" but depending on the oil and your skin's sensitivity, the oils can be diluted with a carrier oil like coconut oil and then applied to the skin.

A second way is to use the oils aromatically. This way is quite convenient and offers benefits immediately. Use your oils aromatically by using an essential oil diffuser, in a spray type mister, or place a drop in your hands, rub together and inhale. The last way is to use essential oils internally. NOT ALL OILS can be used internally and it is important to read the label before using internally.

DoTerra Essential Oils are certified pure therapeutic grade and the majority of their oils can be used internally just simply read the label! This is the only brand of oils I use for many, many reasons but number one is that I know my oils are pure!

You can place a drop or two directly underneath your tongue, have a few drops in your water or use vegetable caps to make an easy to swallow pill.

The first oil I would like to talk about is Lavender. This is one oil I never want to run out of so I make sure to keep a stash! Lavender is most commonly referred to for its calming benefits and helping aide in sleep. Often times when one is stressed, they will experience difficulty sleeping so the calming aroma of lavender aides in that. Drop a few drops on your pillow case so you can aromatically inhale that floral calming scent throughout the night or mix with some Epsom salts and drop into a warm bath before bed. This oil can be taken internally to help ease anxious feelings.

My favorite recipe with lavender is to mix a drop into a tall glass of lemonade! Instantly you will feel relaxed, calm, and mellow. Copaiba essential oil, released last year is relatively new to the market and is derived from the resin of the Copaiba tree found specifically in South America. Copaiba's slightly spicy, woody scent has made it popular in the cosmetics & fragrance industry prior to the release of the oil.

I have found the best way to gain the most benefits from this oil is to use internally. While the taste is not the best, your body will thank you as this oil not only helps to ease those anxious feelings but also supports your immune, cardiovascular, digestive, and respiratory systems and is offered in a soft gel cap for easy internal usage.

The next oil discussed is a blend of several oils specific to only DoTerra. I felt the need to talk about this blend because of the impact it has had on me in regard to my stress and daily life. Balance, the grounding blend is a blend of the following oils – Ho Wood, Spruce, Frankincense, Blue Tansy, Osmanthus and Blue Chamomile with fractionated coconut oil. They deemed this oil blend the "grounding blend" due to the number of oils in it that are derived from trees.

Think about a tree – a tree stands tall with its roots planted firmly into the ground. Without being rooted into the ground, the tree would simply topple over. The woodsy, slightly sweet aroma helps us to "ground" our emotions and live more in the moment. This oil can be used both aromatically and topically.

My favorite use of this oil is to apply the oil directly to the bottoms of my feet each morning which allows me to feel balanced and calm throughout the day.

Using oils on the bottoms of the feet is a quick way to get the oils into the blood stream as the pores on the bottom of your feet are much larger compared to the pores elsewhere on our bodies.

The last oil blend I would like to talk about is also specific to DoTerra but is in my daily arsenal! I never had a difficult time sleeping until recent years dealing with stress from work as well as grief. This blend has allowed me to maintain a bedtime routine the helps me to fall asleep quickly and stay asleep. The blend is called Serenity, the restful blend.

This blend is made up of Lavender, Cedarwood, Ho Wood, Ylang Ylang, Marjoram, Roman Chamomile, Vetiver, Hawaiian Sandalwood, and Vanilla Bean Absolute. This company offers this blend in oil form, in a bath bar, and in soft gel form. I prefer to use the oil and bath bar at night,

 I have found that the soft gels are best to use during the day for anxious feelings that pop up during my day. This oil blend is another one that is great to apply at the bottoms of the feet before bed or adding to Epsom salts for a relaxing bath. the wood oils in this blend (Ho Wood, Cedarwood, and Vetiver) give a grounding benefit as well. Essential oils have given me tools to go to when I am feeling stressed. I have several methods I can use (aromatically, internally or topically) to aide in releasing those anxious and tense feelings. These are just a few of my favorite go-to oils for when I am feeling stressed but there are so many more out there! Explore, research and experiment to find what oils work best in your daily routine and this might change depending on the day and what your body needs.

Suzie loved the idea of essential oils helping with stress. The only problem with that idea, was Suzie had no sense of smell. Wondering if they work even if you can't smell, she went back to Google. www.quora.com gave her the answers.

She found the finding stated that absolutely that you could benefit from oils even if your nose couldn't smell. But only, if what you're using is true essential oil. Whether applied topically, ingested, or inhaled, the essential oils still have the exact same medicinal properties, and your body will react to them the same way, even if you can't sense them. Someone who can't smell may lose some of the psychological effect, but can still experience benefits from using them.

The article referenced a story of a man with severe Parkinson's (Vietnam vet exposed to agent Orange) that caused him to lose his sense of smell. The family was shocked at how he seemed to feel better and cognitively function better when they used a diffuser with lemon and peppermint next to him.

Tied in Knots

Using our Behaviors to Release Stress

Changing our behaviors can result in reducing our stress. Many times, the coping tools we develop are not healthy ones. You may not realize it, but changing behaviors and actions including exercising, getting enough sleep and eating healthy foods are important to your physical health. but also, to your mental and emotional health as well. Think of a time when you didn't get enough sleep because you were working late or binge-watching Netflix and ate junk food and coffee all day.

How did you feel afterwards?

How much more likely were you to get into a fight with your partner or a coworker the next day? When your body doesn't feel well, you're much more likely to feel bad emotionally. Developing positive actions and behaviors for when you are stress will reduce the stress and teach you ways to limit future stress.

Gratitude is a behavior that when practiced regularly, people tend to stress less and take more time to notice and reflect upon the things they're thankful for. They reportedly experience more positive emotions, feel more alive, sleep better, express more compassion and kindness, and even have stronger immune systems

What we think and feel affects how we behave. When people take a positive outlook, they are often nicer to be around. Nothing is more encouraging than feelings of gratitude and acts of kindness towards others.

Stress seems to melt away as the individual focuses on the positive aspects of life and being kind to others. Feeling thankful for life can have a positive self-worth regarding one's overall well-being. Being grateful and showing kindness to others helps us detach ourselves from stress because our focus is now shifted to a positive experience.

Doing this on a regular basis helps put things into perspective, ensuring you only stress out when it is relevant and necessary to do so.

Linda's Story

Kindness is a simple answer in a sometimes difficult and challenging world. I know that to be true. For a long time now, it has been my mission to acknowledge and appreciate all people and to encourage others to do the same.

When my granddaughter Skylar, was young and we'd go out, we had a contest called "Who can make the most people smile?" And we continue it today. It makes for a wonderful glorious day.

We will be in the supermarket and someone will be walking down the aisle with her head down. Skylar walks up to her and gives her a big smile. I watch her walk down the aisle, turn around and smile at Skylar again or perhaps smile at someone else.

Kindness is a chain that pulls us all together. Anything that lifts another person is kindness. Every single act of kindness has a ripple effect.

In 2002, my dad had a series of strokes and other illness. At that time, I was the facilitator for a large women's networking organization. One day I asked the ladies if on a personal level, they could send their positive energies my dad's way and maybe go out and do something nice for someone, someone for whom they would not normally think to do something nice.

My dad has been doing nice things for all sorts of people for years, from the street crossing guard, to the waitress in a restaurant, to a friend's mother. That same day, I made cookies for the janitor at the post office. When I gave him the cookies, he actually looked a little embarrassed.

"Why, Linda?" he asked "

"Because I appreciate you!" I answered. "When I get here at 6am and it is still dark out and it is a little scary, I know you are inside and I feel safe. And when I first moved here and my post office box was always empty, you always cheered me on. And you keep this place spotless."

That evening his wife called me and said that he was overwhelmed. "No one even knows his name never minds bakes him cookies! What can I do for you?" she asked "Nothing, just go out and do something nice for someone else." I answered.

Well, that woman and many other women started practicing kindness on a regular basis. It was wonderful to witness. After that day, I started becoming more and more aware of the kindnesses in this wonderful world of ours. In fact, a few weeks later, I was in a drugstore looking at some items when I noticed three people standing on line at the prescription counter. The last person was a young woman with a crying baby. It was obvious the baby was sick.

When she got to the head of the line, the pharmacist said he was sorry but they did not have that medication on hand but that they could get it in about 2 hours. One tear just trickled down the young woman's cheek.

Suddenly an older gentleman who was sitting on the side came over and asked if he could be of assistance. The young woman looked up at him bewildered. The man said that he didn't have much to do and that he had to wait for his prescription, so if she wanted, he could deliver her prescription to her home. "But I don't even know you," she said. "I won't come in your house," he replied. "I'll just leave it by the door and ring the bell. "

"But why?" she asked.

The man looked at her with kind eyes and said, "I live on a really limited income and my children, grandchildren and great grandchildren all live up north and I rarely get to see them so this would a privilege for me. "

With that, people in the store started nodding their heads to the young woman with approval. She mumbled okay, wrote her address on a piece of paper and gave it to the man. The baby stopped crying and the young woman left the store. By that time, I was crying. I walked over to the gentleman, introduced myself and told him how wonderful it was that he was so kind.

Michael was 82 years old. We became friends and had breakfast and lunch a few times.

About three months later, he phoned me to tell me that the young woman had told all of her friends about what he had done by delivering the prescription. They all chipped in and sent him airfare to visit his family. Another wonderful act of kindness and it was the last time Michael saw his family before he died.

When I am having a tough day, I recall this total act of unsolicited kindness and it always brings to me waves of gratitude. We are surrounded by kindness every day. Unfortunately, we get so wrapped in life that we forget to stop and smell the roses, as they say, or witness the acts of kindness that surround us each day. Little acts of kindness and love are the best parts of one's life.

As the Dalai Lama said, "When we feel love and kindness toward others, it not only makes others feel loved and cared for, but it helps us to develop inner happiness and peace. "So, get out today and experience the kindness around you. Bathe in it and be kind to others. You may discover that being kind to others is actually being kind to yourself.

Volunteering may be good for body and mind, but it also can reduce stress. I already knew about the mental health benefits of volunteering. Studies have shown that volunteering helps people who donate their time feel more socially connected, thus warding off loneliness and depression. I was however surprised to learn that volunteering has positive implications that go beyond mental health. www.helpguide.org suggests that people who give their time to others might also be rewarded with better health—including lower blood pressure, reduced stress and a longer lifespan.

Evidence of volunteerism's physical effects can be found in a recent study published in Psychology and Aging. Adults over age 50 who volunteered on a regular basis were less likely to develop high blood pressure than non-volunteers.

High blood pressure, often caused by stress, is an important indicator of one's health because it contributes to heart disease, stroke, and premature death. Lowering stress also helps by boosting self-confidence —especially for older adults

"Performing volunteer work could increase physical activity among people who aren't otherwise very active and may also reduce stress. "Many people find volunteer work to be helpful with respect to stress reduction, and we know that stress is very strongly linked to health outcomes," says Rodlescia Sneed, a doctoral candidate in social and health psychology at Carnegie Mellon University.

Studies have found a health benefit from as little as 100 hours of volunteering a year or 2 hours a week One key for achieving health benefits from volunteering is to do it for the right reasons. A 2012 study in the journal "Health Psychology" found that participants who volunteered with some regularity lived longer, but only if their intentions were truly altruistic. Volunteer to help others— not to make yourself feel better.

The Greek philosopher Aristotle once surmised that the essence of life is "To serve others and do good." If recent research is any indication, serving others might also be the essence of good health. Volunteering makes an immeasurable difference in the lives of others. But did you know how much you help yourself by giving back?

By savoring your time spent in service to others, you'll feel a sense of meaning and appreciation—both given and received—which can be calming and reduce stress levels. Experience "The Happiness Effect." You know that feel-good sense you get after a vigorous workout? It comes from a release of dopamine in the brain. Helping others has that exact same effect—so the more you volunteer, the happier you become!

Ron's story

Stress, what stress? My chosen profession was in the area of finance and accounting. Pretty boring, right? No stress, just crunching numbers. There was a lot of stress! First, payrolls had to be met every week; when Friday rolled around, employees expected their payroll check. Bills had to be paid; vendors who provided goods and services expected to receive compensation for those goods or services. No pay, no more goods.

As I was working and learning finance and accounting, technology was changing. Payroll departments were being "computerized." Jobs were changing. Education was changing. We were changing. There was a lot of stress.

How I dealt with stress in the early days was through physical exercise. I would make sure to take a lunch break that involved jogging or pumping iron or swimming. Getting out of the office seemed to be a good idea. Doing something physical seemed to be a good idea and it worked for me.

It seemed like the stress would never go away, though. There was always a new "app"; always something "more" was needed. This was the age of information technology. In order to do more, we had to learn more. In order to learn more, we had to take more classes. Taking more classes led to studying for tests and writing papers - more stress.

What I did learn quickly was to get organized. That was helpful in avoiding stress. Planning ahead became really important, not only for work and school, but family time. Taking time off to spend time with the family is important and should be a stress reliever. It isn't, you stress about the job when you're not on the job. So, planning for a vacation had to be planned into the job. As I matured, I realized that a lot of stress could be avoided by communication. First, understanding what is wanted. Then communicating back that understanding. "This is what I think you want, is that right?" Good.

Next step, creating a project plan. Reviewing the project plan, tweaking the plan, etc. Frequent review of the plan as it was being executed. Hit a snag? Need something?

Communicating is key to success and avoiding stress. That's the theory, anyway. Well, that's how I spent my 40-year career. Now that I'm retired, I shouldn't have any stress, right? I could sit home and watch TV and drink beer and the only stress would be.... running out of beer? But no, I like to keep busy, so I find things to do. I have always liked to sing and have wanted to perform on stage.

I have found and performed with different groups and most recently, the Matinee Opera Players. The Players don't do a full opera, they sing songs from famous operas, sing some show tunes and I get to sing a "popular" song or two.

What could be stressful?

Well, performing can be stressful. But I have somehow become the manager of this group and things need to get done. The performance space has to be reserved, seating plans created, the program planned and get it all organized into a program book.

The program book has to be printed which cost money, so how about selling ads in the program to offset the cost? How about marketing and advertising? How do we get the word out so people will come to the show?

It can be stressful getting the shows together and it usually is. I have found that to avoid stress, its best to keep those communication channels open just like when I was working. Planning is just as important in putting a show together as it is implementing a new financial system. How do I manage the stress? Same as before: some physical exercise, engaging socially with my "customers" and having a plan. Good planning is a great way to avoid stress.

Suzie always told herself that she didn't have time to volunteer. After reading about the many benefits in doing so, she decided to look into it. While watching television one evening, she saw a place she may like to volunteer. Her mother lived with her now, and Suzie provides all her meals.

She had discovered that unlike her mother, many seniors in her community live alone and due to medical or financial reasons, are unable to fix their own food. Neighborly Senior Services offers a program called "Meals on Wheels" that might be the answer. In giving just a few hours a week of her time, she could make someone's life a bit easier. Seeing the smiles on the faces of those she visited resulted in a smile on her face and in her heart.

Out with bad habits. If you are prone to stress, look at your habits, you may need to begin to eliminate some of the bad ones to improve your mental health. Sometimes it is necessary to eliminate old habits before newer, more positive habits can be implemented.

Steer clear of people who are hurtful and unkind. You're not obliged to socialize with people who don't treat you with care and respect, even if they're related to you. Minimize the time you spend with people whose company you don't enjoy, and seek out more time with those you do. Do you drink excessively and smoke? Often these two habits are thought to be coping tools, however, they can also make matters worse.

Many smokers believe that tobacco helps them cope with stress. But while they may feel calmer and less stressed while smoking, their bodies are experiencing just the opposite reactions.

Some other potentially destructive habits to avoid include sleeping too much, becoming angry when stressed, avoiding your problems, and bingeing on low-nutrient foods.

As much as Suzie hated to admit it, in the past, she had tended to gravitate towards bad coping habits before utilizing the good ones. Before understanding the positive ways to reduce and manage her stress, she would often use food as a coping tool. This is not uncommon. Since childhood, many of us have been rewarded with food. When crying or misbehaving, we are offered a cookie or lollipop if we behave and be quiet. We are told if we finish our dinner, we can have dessert. When we celebrate something happy, it usually involves food. When we gather following a funeral, we eat over our sadness.

Suzie realized that many of her emotions were responded to with food. The sugar, the crunchy and salty snacks seemed to comfort her. In reality, she was harming her body. Never could she remember or feel the urge to eat broccoli when stressed!

Do you eat when you are stressed, frustrated or angry?

Research has shown that small changes like switching to whole grain bread would help with stress. Rather than fluffy white bread, which has little nutrition, the whole grain helps speed amino acids to the brain which increases the serotonin levels in our brain.

This increase in serotonin levels help us to relax.

Suzie discovered changing her eating habits didn't have to be drastic. When designing her stress management diet, adding some fruits and vegetables such as having a salad provided needed nutrition and fiber. Choosing fresh food over processed food and learning to introduce fish and lean meats into her diet at least once a week. Switching from soda to water would save her many calories a day and was so much healthier to drink. She was shocked to learn one twelve-ounce soda had eight grams of sugar in it.

Some days she had consumed almost her daily allotment of sugar just on soda! If the sugar discovery was bad enough, the caffeine also drained the vitamin B from her body. What could she do to improve her eating that would also help reduce her stress?

A healthy body responds better to the inevitable stress of life than one with poor eating choices. Good nutrition is the building block of good health. Eating well can prevent you from having high blood pressure, heart disease, indigestion, diabetes, and obesity.

Some of the foods you should limit or eliminate from your life are unhealthy fats, sugar, salt and caffeine. Eating a variety of food filled with more complex carbohydrate and fiber can be the start of developing a food plan. Only you have the power to take charge of your eating habits.

Learning to identify emotional eating and having a food plan can show that taking charge can make a positive difference in stress reduction.

When something would cause her to feel stressed, including eating the wrong foods or eating too much, she would get on the computer and surf the internet or play a "mindless" game. The games did take her mind off of what was stressing her out. The problem was, when she stopped the distraction, the stress returned.

Bad habits interrupted and prevented her from accomplishing positive goals and finding constructive solutions to her stress. Most of the time, bad habits are simply a way of avoiding dealing with stress and boredom. But it doesn't have to be that way. You can teach yourself new and healthy ways to deal with stress and monotony, which you can then substitute in place of your bad habits. Because bad habits often provide some type of benefit in your life, it's very difficult to simply eliminate them.

This is why simplistic advice like "just stop doing it" rarely works. Instead, you need to replace a bad habit with a new habit that provides a similar benefit.

Suzie admitted she had some bad habits. Whenever she would get stressed, she would often eat something unhealthy. Knowing it was a bad choice, she also realized that to just stop making those choices was unrealistic. Instead, coming up with a different way to deal with stress and learn to insert that new behavior into my life instead of resorting to old poor choices.

During her research, Suzie discovered stressful eating is common. Have you ever noticed how stress makes you hungry? It's not just in your mind. When stress is chronic, as it so often is in our chaotic, fast-paced world, your body produces high levels of the stress hormone, cortisol.

Cortisol triggers cravings for salty, sweet, and fried foods—foods that give you a burst of energy and pleasure. The more you feel your stress is in your life, the more likely you are to turn to food for emotional relief. Choose a substitute for your bad habit. Have a plan ahead of time for how to respond when facing the stress or boredom that prompts your bad habit.

What are you going to do when you get the urge to smoke or eat something unhealthy? (Example: breathing exercises instead.) Whatever it is and whatever you're dealing with, you need to have a plan for what you will do instead of your bad habit.

• Cut out as many triggers as possible. If you smoke when you drink, then don't go to the bar. If you eat cookies when they are in the house, then throw them all away. If the first thing you do when you sit on the couch is pick up the TV remote, then hide the remote in a closet in a different room.

• Make it easier on yourself to break bad habits by avoiding the things that cause them.

• Join forces with somebody. How often do you try to diet in private? Instead, pair up with someone and work together. The two of you can hold each other accountable and celebrate your victories together. Knowing that someone else expects you to be better is a powerful motivator.

• Visualize yourself succeeding. See yourself throwing away the cigarettes or buying healthy food or waking up early. Whatever the bad habit is that you are looking to break, visualize yourself crushing it, smiling, and enjoying your success.

Talking to someone. Sometimes all someone really needs is for someone else to listen to them. When feeling overwhelmed, a supportive voice can help you calm down and re-assure you everything will be fine. Supportive, positive relationships allow you to feel as though you are cared for and have someone to rely on. For instance, if you are overly stressed out about work, meet up with a friend.

Talk about the challenges you are facing, and they can help put things into perspective. Surround yourself with people who have your best interests in mind, if no one is around, try talking to yourself. Sometimes all you need to do is to slow your thoughts down, prioritize your tasks, and assure yourself everything will be okay.

Baran's Story

Words exchanged between one another seem so simple yet it's so complicated when it's with the wrong person. That wrong person creates stress and puts you in such uncomfortable situations that when you try to explain the downfalls that occurred throughout the day, they become ignorant and occupied.

I approached the one person that would hear me out regardless of the bizarre story I created in my head. I opened the door, sat on the chair and just glanced at my surroundings. I took in the beige sandpaper walls, the ocean view outside the window that put me at peace, and most importantly at the petite woman with crystal glasses starting intently back at me. I took in a deep breath and did not really know where to begin. Do I start from the beginning, should I just start where it really bothers me, or should I just let her start? These thoughts kept circling around in my head, and I felt her waiting for me to start.

I was about to fumble out my thoughts, biting my tongue on what to say when she whispered, "Breathe and just start with what you're thinking right now".

That sentence is all I needed to hear before I start my mini novel of stress created situations and drown out the noise coming from the restaurants near us.

An hour passes by and I feel like my tongue ran a marathon. After I take one last deep breath, I look up at her waiting for the criticism, and opinions that are about to attack me. Except there were no opinions, there were just questions, genuine concern.

I felt relieved

She actually listened. Someone actually listened to me and did not judge me. She grabbed my hand and told me that all these things I just talked about are not going to be fixed quickly, that our time together did not fix things at that moment, but that it fixed my mindset, and relieved my stress.

My stress levels went down tremendously and I actually felt like I was able to do anything. Like if I were to jump off a cliff, I would be able to fly with the amount of confidence I gained in passing my stress off to someone who actually cared.

As I was about to approach the door, and say goodbye to my stress reliever, I was already coming up with plans on how to fix my situations, and how to be happy again.

I could not have done it without someone listening to me and actually hearing me out, even if it didn't do anything at the moment. Sometimes all you need is someone to listen to you.

Decluttering your life Looking around her crowded and messy house, Suzie let out a long sigh. The clutter made her feel stressed and She always wanted a more organized living area but didn't really know where to start. She was raised in the home of her hoarding mother who taught her to never get rid of anything.

Suzie remembered several times in her childhood that her mother said "Don't throw that away, you might need it again". When she tried to declutter, she became depressed and just gave up. Watching a television show about letting go of the things she no longer found pleasing, she decided to do it herself. Since she was working on finding ways to reduce her stress, and clutter was making her stressed, it seemed the perfect time.

The television shows where people come in, clean, and make everything look beautiful and neat in an hour or two is deceiving. Decluttering takes time, and can be extremely emotional. The first question to ask yourself is why you have kept an item for this long.

In the closet, back behind the clothes she no longer wore was a box her favorite aunt had sent her. Inside the box was a large bowl with a matching salt and pepper shakers that all looked like cabbage. She laughed even now thinking how her friends would also chuckle at the site of such a unique table accessory. Her mother had mailed it to her when she got married and moved away. They had used it every Easter dinner to put coleslaw in. Now that her aunt had passed away, it was an emotional memory of days gone by.

The book on decluttering reminded her, to get rid of an unusual item is not getting rid of the person who gave it to us or the special memories you shared. You may feel sad and even shed a few tears as you decide what to get rid of and what to keep. Suzie knew she had several small trinkets that belonged to her mother and were special to her. Keeping one box of special items will reduce the clutter but not leave you feeling abandoned.

Do you ever feel guilty after you purchased something expensive and then never wore it? You are not alone. Looking at the red high heels in her closet she frowned. Normally they were extremely expensive, and even at 50% off she could have paid a bill or two. She never wore them, not once. In her mind she would be invited to a fancy party and arrive with her red shoes gleaming.

Maybe someone gave you a gift that you really didn't love, so it went into the dark corners of your closet. Keeping these items will not make you feel better or less stressed, it could even make you feel worse. Give them away or sell them to someone else who can use them. You will feel lighter, proud of yourself, and calmer.

Is your tablet or phone filled with Pinterest photos of items or ideas that you planned to have in your home one day? Waiting until you have time and money to make them will never happen unless to make it happen. Pick a few and just do it! Be proud of your new accomplishment, the addition to your home, and more room on your electronics.

As Suzie's mom had told her, you might need it one day has kept me holding onto clothing. Buying a dress, I loved that was a bit snug, I told myself it would inspire me to lose weight. That didn't happen, in fact, I felt depressed as that dress reminded me of yet another failed attempt to stick to a diet.

One of my friends joked they have three different sizes of clothes hanging in their closet. Wishful clothes they hoped to wear one day, like my dress. Current clothes she wears now, and "fat" clothes in case she gains weight or want to feel extra comfortable. Get rid of the excess clothes! Think of the charity that can benefit from them or the woman who will have the same rush of excitement felt by you when you first purchased them.

Having a more organized home is just one of the benefits of decluttering your life. You may also have more energy.

When Suzie looked around her house, she saw clutter everywhere. Dishes piled in the sink and clothes unfolded and tumbling out of the baskets. Looking around left her feeling overwhelmed, yet she laid on the sofa and did nothing about them.

When your house is cluttered you may eat more and be less productive at work as your mind can also become less cluttered. The benefits of decluttering may surprise you.

As mentioned, decluttering doesn't happen in an hour or two. It takes time. Saying you wish you could declutter is the first step, and making a plan to do so is the second step. Start small by setting aside fifteen minutes or an hour towards a less crowded and stressful life. Set realistic goals and stick to them. Seeing how doing so will reduce cleaning time, free up space in your home and become less stressed. As with any change we, as humans take on, we have to want it to happen.

Mary Jane's Story

Needing to work to support my family, I continued to work with overloaded stress. My denial resulted in me ignoring the warning signs of stress until I faced a full-blown burnout. I ignored the small signs such as no longer looking forward to going to work and feeling irritability towards others. I also ignored the larger signs such as changes in my physical and emotional well-being.

I had been working as a counselor for over ten years and could conceive remaining with the company until retirement age. The journey of my work history with the company went from both management and myself feeling satisfied with my performance, to one of my feeling unhappy and stressed.

I ignored the warning signs and had blinders on as leadership began to question my performance and I became worried. Unbeknown to me at the time, middle management had been told to "thin out the staff". They were instructed to find the flaws of staff members and put pressure on them to leave the company.

Feeling I was the only one being targeted resulted in daily fears of losing my job. For nine years my reviews had been positive and a yearly raise was always awarded to me. But things had begun to change.

As a result of the pressure, I started questioning my abilities, second guessing my decisions, and I started being tearful at work.

Speaking to a human resource employee and my leadership team appeared to be even more damaging to my security and left me feeling vulnerable.

With those blinders on, I was asked to compromise my actions and current role with the company.

I ignored my feelings and how work was affecting me until it was too late. I didn't talk about the situation with anyone else for fear it would make me appear weak to co-workers and even more vulnerable to management.

Finally, in total burnout mode, I requested to take a leave of absence to regroup and heal myself.

My leave of absence began with three months' time off work and it was suggested I attend an EAP or employee assistance counselor.

During the eight weeks of attending counseling we discussed what happened to me at work and how it made me feel. In talking with the counselor, I discovered the stress and pressure I felt had resulted in a lack of confidence in my own ability to do my job. Counseling was continued and a second three months off was suggested. Human resource now listed me as being on short-term disability, which guaranteed me a position when I returned, but not necessarily the one I had before my time off.

While on my leave of absence, I began talking with co-workers, and I discovered, I was not the only one being "picked on". There were about twenty employees who were also placed in different positions or asked to resign.

Speaking to a fellow co-worker who was also a victim of management's pressure, she told me she had experienced the same emotional and physical reaction as I did, and like me, from emotional stress, had chosen to leave the company.

> The outcome of your stress does not have to be a negative one like mine, there is good news.

In sharing my tale of work stress, I do not want to give the impression that I was totally blameless. When suffering from this type of stress you are affected physically, emotionally, and your thoughts may be scattered or you may have trouble concentrating.

Stress did affect my performance, but in offering help and support, rather than the tactics used, they could have kept an experienced employee, and I may still be working for them.

Rather than denying what is happening to you due to work stress, work on ways to reduce or manage the stress before you experience a meltdown. Learn to be aware of the subtle and quiet messages your body is telling you.

Noticing when you are beginning to feel overwhelmed is the first step toward stopping an emotional meltdown before it happens.

You may experience feelings of embarrassment after an emotional outburst, but this is a normal reaction and shows we are human, I was no exception. I was embarrassed that stress had resulted in my inability to work. If I had broken a leg or suffered from an illness, no one would question my respite from working.

Having to leave due to emotional reasons, I felt like a failure and "less than" to those who continue to do the same job as I had. When others learned it was due to stress burnout, I believed they thought I was weak and I scrambled to justify myself.

An emotional meltdown may begin by someone crying uncontrollably or finding yourself feeling like snapping at others or lashing out angrily. For some people it may involve the "fight or flight" feeling and they find themselves in a panic or want to run away from a stressful situation.

Accepting my situation, following months of EAP counseling, I began to focus my energy on understanding what happened to me. The effects of burnout had transformed me, physically and emotionally and psychologically.

My task now was now to learn how I could prevent another workplace meltdown from happening to me. What I learned was that meltdowns or burnouts can happen from stress at work, home, or in your personal life. To avoid potentially having a meltdown, you must begin to look at your life. Have you taken on too much work or family obligations?

Taking on too many responsibilities all at once or agreeing to too many activities are a surefire recipe for stress. As your obligations begin to mount, you start to begin feeling overwhelmed and building the foundation for a potential meltdown. You can't stop difficult situations from occurring, but you can learn how to change your response to them.

The Benefit of Taking Care of Yourself

Many of us are incredibly hard on ourselves, expecting results that we would never expect from our family or friends. Being critical of ourselves is sometimes needed, but it is also important to give ourselves some credit. If you are overly stressed out about something, try to focus on the big picture. Remember a time when you completed a challenging or stressful task. Remind yourself that you can overcome this situation.

Giving yourself a "pat on the back" once in a while, can help you re-energize, focus, and practice self-compassion.

Home stress, life stress, and even work stress are a part of our lives. Most of us do not have a choice but to work at a job, but we don't have to let this stress us out. Developing techniques to guard against stress affecting us negatively, can result in increased performance and productivity at work.

Using these tools can improve our self-esteem and reduce self-doubt giving us a more positive outlook.

Learning ways to reduce stress can also result in improved health. At least once a week, listen to music or read a book unrelated to your work. Take hourly breaks at work and breathe deeply.

Many workers reported they ate at their desk or skipped lunch. Instead, sit down and chew your food slowly. Take time to taste and enjoy each bite.

Develop friendships where you have nothing to gain, but rather enjoy each other's company reduces stress. When we are healthier emotionally, we tend to have less resentment when asked for help from others and be a more willing listener.

What are some ways to take better care of yourself?

It all comes down to ATTITUDE!

Don't sweat the small stuff. Make life a bit easier

- Get up 15 minutes earlier each day

- Prepare for the morning the night before

- Never wear tight-fitting clothes or shoes

- Don't rely on your memory, use your planner to remember tasks & meetings

- Make duplicates of keys • 	Leave for work a little earlier

- Laugh- a 10 second belly laugh equaled 10 minutes on a rowing machine in the raising of one's heart rate (exercise reduces stress)

- Live life with a passion- in your work, friends, hobbies and your life Celebrate...whatever! Surround yourself with happy people.

- Getting to a happier, less stressed place in life does not have to be difficult. However, it does mean that you are willing to change.

- Turn negative patterns of behavior that once triggered poor choices into positive decisions. To reduce stress, you must create balance in your life. Balance between work and play, being with others and being alone, and activity and rest.

> You need to be able to manage stress because hard times will come, and a positive outlook is what gets you through.
> Marie Osmond

Be willing to listen to and respond to the communication that takes place in your thoughts, feelings, your brain and physical body. it's important to note that you can't just talk yourself out of stress or "tough it out" and resort to distractions.

Be gentle with yourself as you adjust and implement new behaviors and conditions. Allow rest time between commitments and find time for fun and relaxing.

The important thing to remember is stress reducing options have to work for you. If they stress you out, don't do them. What works for one person may be totally wrong for another. The effects of stress tend to build up over time.

Taking practical steps to manage your stress can reduce or prevent these effects. Change happens, and it often stresses us out. The challenge is to accept that change happens and go with the flow and enjoy your life, rather than fight it

The suggestions and information gathered in this journal are not designed to replace treatment. Talk to Your Doctor or Health Care Provider. Get proper health care for existing or new health concerns. Contact a counselor if desiring treatment.

When you recover or discover something
that nourishes your soul and brings joy,
care enough about yourself to make
room for it in your life."

– Jean Shinoda Bolen

"In Closing

Finishing her research, Suzie began thinking of her stress, her symptoms, and what she could do to reduce that stress. She now knew the physical and emotional signs that she was getting stressed, and things that could prevent it from escalating.

When her mind started getting filled with worry and self-doubt, she turned on some music she liked and took a deep breath. Slowly breathing in and out to the beat of her relaxing music she found herself relaxing as well.

Although not a morning person by nature, Suzie started setting her alarm for one hour earlier than usual. This was her hour, her time to do whatever she wanted.

Feeling the need to do everything for others was one of her triggers, and she now knew her needs were just as important. In fact, she smiled, she may be even more important. The saying, "You cannot pour from an empty well" means if she doesn't take care of herself, she can't help others.

Sometimes she walked her neighborhood with her newly rescued dog Layla. Taking the time for this walk, Suzie was able to look at the world with new eyes. Running with Layla on other days, she got exercise and found she enjoyed and even look forward to those days as much as Layla did. Taking life, a bit slower, at her own chosen pace, she found those stress-filled moments began to decline.

Feeling calmer these days, Suzie is able to face the unfortunate and always present stress-filled events, without worry and reduced stress using one of the suggestions she learned.

Recourses

https://www.apa.org/helpcenter/understanding-chronic-stress.aspx

https://www.apa.org/helpcenter/stress-kinds.aspx

https://www.heartmath.org/articles-of-the-heart/science-of-the-heart/stress-and-cognitive-decline/

https://www.stress.org/workplace-stress/

https://healthnet.com/portal/home/content/iwc/home/articles/Tips_to_Reduce_Stress_at_Home.action

www.mindbodygreen.com

www.selfgrowth.com

www.psychologytoday.com/us/blog/the-myth-stress

The Stress Solution by Lyle H. Miller, PhD, and Alma Dell Smith, PhD.

Anderson, N.B. & Anderson, P.E. (2003). Emotional Longevity: what really determines how long you live. New York: Viking.

https://health.howstuffworks.com/wellness/diet-fitness/exercise/benefits-of-walking5.htm

http://createthegood.org/articles/volunteeringhealth

https://www.health.harvard.edu/blog/volunteering-may-be-good-for-body-and-mind-201306266428

https://jamesclear.com/how-to-break-a-bad-habit

https://www.everydayhealth.com/wellness/united-states-of-stress/

http://socialpsychonline.com/2015/11/psychology-ostracism-feeling-excluded/

Thank you for purchasing my book, Tied in Knots 3
Steps to Releasing Stress. If journaling is something
you or a loved one feels may be useful, visit my
website for a free download of this book's
workbook. If you found this information helpful, I
invite you to leave your review on Amazon.

www.maryjanecronin.com

About the Author

Mary Jane Cronin has over 16 years of experience
counseling individuals and groups dealing with stress
from grief, work life balance, and unexpected changes
in our lives. A native of New Jersey, she left the Jersey
shores for the Florida beaches and has lived in the
Tampa Bay area for 40 years. She joined Toastmasters
in 2015, where she earned an Advanced Gold
Communication award.

Mary enjoys speaking to groups about self-care when
dealing with changes in family or work life. She
lectures and has taught support skills to teenagers,
incarcerated women, hospice patients and their
families, as well as to hospice volunteers, and fellow
health care professionals.

Her passion to help people reclaim the emotional balance in their lives motivated her to publish her books, Tied in Knots is Mary Jane's sixth book. Her writing career began following the death of her son, when she wrote and published November Mourning.

Mary Jane, a licensed mental health counselor earned her Bachelor's Degree in Human Development from Eckerd College in St Petersburg, Florida, and her Master's Degree in Community Psychology from Springfield College in Springfield, Massachusetts. Ms. Cronin was employed in the health care field for ten years. Following her departure, she opened her private practice where she offers counseling, coaching, and professional speaking.

CONNECT WITH MARY JANE ON SOCIAL MEDIA

https://twitter.com/CounselorMary

https://www.facebook.com/maryjanecronin1

linkedin.com/in/mary-jane-cronin-63a957101

YouTube/Counselor Mary Jane

Other Books by Mary Jane Cronin

November Mourning

Mary Jane Cronin has written not just a fact- filled book about loss and grief, but one that included her personal journey to understand, accept and heal following the 1998 murder of her own son. November Mourning offers insight and hope as it explores the emotions parents feel following the loss of a child.

Travel with Mary Jane through the stages of grief and develop techniques to help move through them easier. Discover what other parents have said and done to help reduce their own suffering.

ISBN: 978-0615239781

Writing Through Your Grief

Writing Through your Grief is a guidebook to help you through a loss. Losing someone you love is difficult. Trying to continue in a world without them is even more difficult. Writing Through your Grief offers you an opportunity to reflect on your time together, your emotions and the way you have dealt with grief in the past. Through the writing prompts, you will share stories, and learn about the healing process. Although you will never be "over" it, it is my hope you will one day be able to smile when you share stories about them … rather than fill with tears.

ISBN: 978-0984501601

A Caregiver's Connection

We are living longer these days. The result is often a loved one faced with illness and limitations requiring a caregiver to step in and help with their care. Many are also taking on this role with little or no training and knowledge of what to do. A Caregiver's Connection offers resources, and self-care ideas for the caregivers.

ISBN: 978-0984501625

Unexpected Change

We often fear change, resist it, and even try to avoid it from happening. We begin to accept change when we have control of it. In this book you will learn there are several factors that determine our response to inevitable changes and what you can do to be able to accept and adapt to change. ISBN: 9780984501632

Growing Through Illness Together

When someone you love is diagnosed with a terminal illness or disease there are many unanswered questions. Growing Through Illness Together is an informative yet personal guide of what to expect. Filled with medical facts with just enough personal stories it helped the reader understand the steps that happen not only to the person diagnosed, but also to the caregiver, spouse, and loved ones. The tips and advice given on how to move forward is inspiring and comforting. ISBN: 978-0-9845016-4-9

Tied in Knots

Tied in Knots

www.ingramcontent.com/pod-product-compliance
Lightning Source LLC
Chambersburg PA
CBHW070758100426
42742CB00012B/2184